An Illustrated History of

L.M.S.
WAGONS

Frontispiece Toton, 6th July 1927. This picture, taken when the LMS was but 4½ years old, is remarkable if only for the total absence of wagons in pre-grouping livery. The majority of the vehicles carrying LMS insignia are of Midland origin and without doubt the most interesting is the 10 ton goods brake van, the left hand vehicle of the pair standing in front of the signal box. This is only the second example of one of these vehicles to be seen by the author carrying evidence of LMS ownership and still in revenue service. The running number appears to be M729.

Photograph British Rail courtesy National Railway Museum

An Illustrated History of
L.M.S.
WAGONS

by R.J. Essery

Volume One

Originally published by the Oxford Publishing Co. 1981. ISBN 86093 127 7.
Paperback edition published by Kevin Robertson (Noodle Books) 2010
ISBN 978 1 906419 33 2

Just prior to publication, this picture came to light, and so the opportunity has been taken to include this view of the single example of the convertible sheep & cattle wagon built to D1818, described on page 26.

Photograph C. Yates Collection

Printed by The Information Press

Published (2010) by:

Kevin Robertson (Noodle Books)
PO Box 279
Corhampton
SOUTHAMPTON
Hants
SO32 3ZX

www.noodlebooks.co.uk

The Publishers wish to point out that many of the drawings are not of a high quality but are genuine reproductions from the original drawings.

AUTHOR'S NOTES

In 1963, when the LMS Society had just been formed, I met for the first time the late W. O. Steel and together we began to record the vast subject of freight stock in general and LMS standard and pre-group stock in particular, in the firm belief that, one day, the hobby would equal our interest into this aspect of railway operation. In due course, in conjunction with Don Rowland, we produced the first of the modern volumes dealing with freight stock and it is most gratifying to note the number of times *British Goods Wagons* appears as a basic source for reference material.

Since then, many more volumes have appeared dealing with GWR and LNER stock, together with the joint effort of K. R. Morgan and myself which covered LMS standard vehicles. It was before this was published that OPC asked me if I would write the history of the wagons of the Midland Railway and these volumes appeared in 1980 taking the story of Derby Carriage & Wagon works up to 1923. My publisher then suggested that the story should be continued, using the same house style to develop the story of LMS standard stock until nationalization but the difficulty was to present this in an acceptable form within the confines of two volumes.

Previous volumes have tended to group together the same basic types of vehicles into descriptive chapters and for a while this seemed the way it should be written but, thinking about the early days, I decided to discard this idea and to go back to the grass roots and present the work in the form in which it was originally researched.

In 1963, there was no 'guide to researching goods wagons' and I didn't really have any idea of how to begin. It seemed to me that the best way would be to assemble as many pictures and drawings as possible and then to see what an analysis of the material would produce. Therefore, I obtained, through the courtesy of the PRO at Euston, copies of the Freight Wagons, Special Wagons and Container diagram books and photocopied each page. This gave me a copy of these three valuable documents. Then, in conjunction with Bill Steel, we purchased and copied every picture we could find and assembled them into the book by the relevant diagrams. Next, using the lot list which gave general arrangement references, we were able to detect trends and these 'illustrated diagram books' never cease to fascinate visitors who examine them.

And so I decided to present these two volumes as an illustrated diagram book, with each diagram reduced to 4mm scale, as many different photographs as possible and summary of running numbers and livery. If readers find that no pictures or written descriptions exist for particular vehicles or vehicles in certain liveries or conditions, then regrettably, no examples have ever been found, otherwise, thanks to the generosity of my publisher, I have been able to cover fully this vast subject of LMS standard freight stock.

R. J. Essery,
Orpington,
Kent.
1981

Shunting wartime traffic at Chilwell in 1943.
Photograph War Office

INTRODUCTION

The LMS was, in 1923, the largest of the four groups of companies brought about by the 1921 Act which sought to reduce the number of private railway companies from more than 120 to four major groups, excepting a very few which remained outside this amalgamation.

While all the major constituents of the LMS had their own wagon works and designers, it was one company which almost totally influenced future design policy for this giant railway company. As with locomotives and coaches, it was the Midland Railway whose policies were paramount and, apart from starting a new series of lot numbers from No. 1 in 1924, matters continued on their Midland course. 1923 saw the construction of the vehicles ordered in 1922 by the constituent companies and when these orders were complete new LMS designs, which were either standard Midland designs or developments thereof, were produced and so matters remained until nationalization.

Unlike all previous works dealing with freight stock, these volumes have been produced to give readers the opportunity of seeing what could have existed if the railway company had sought to illustrate and provide written information for their employees. Diagram books are just that. They are not working drawings but they do give all the basic dimensions and, as such, provide an easy form of reference for the reader. One can easily recognise certain types although in many instances (covered goods vans are a good example) it is only the running numbers which enable the reader to identify the particular diagram or relate it to actual freight stock.

These volumes, therefore, are laid out as the original diagram books and, in addition to the diagram, there are as many different photographs as possible, as well as livery and running number details which enable the information to be expanded beyond what was available to railway employees.

Because the LMS was highly standardized, it is possible for modellers to build most of these vehicles from the diagrams which can be used in conjunction with the underframe drawings specially drawn for this book and which are featured in *Volume Two*. However, the drawing references given with the diagrams and obtained from the official lot list, will be of value if and when copies of these official general arrangement drawings become available.

In conclusion, I would like to record my appreciation to those who have helped with this project, in particular to John Edgington for obtaining those elusive pictures from the NRM at York. That there will be errors is certain, but they are mine alone and, hopefully, I have been able to expand the story of LMS wagons so that modellers will have plenty to work at in the future.

INDEX OF LMS WAGON STOCK

INDEX OF LMS WAGON STOCK (Cont'd)

INDEX OF LMS WAGON STOCK (Cont'd)

D1656 20 TON GOODS BRAKE VAN

Reclassified by BR as 20 ton Freight Brake Van

Drawing No. 5944   **Figure 1**

These vehicles marked the first change from the original MR design by introducing side duckets — a feature not to be found on that railway before 1923.

100 vehicles were built at Derby 1926/7 to lot 242 and, as noted on the diagram, all were fitted with automatic vacuum brakes.

The numbers were random and Nos. 277, 542, 2045 and 281197 are typical.

Two plates have been selected to illustrate this diagram.

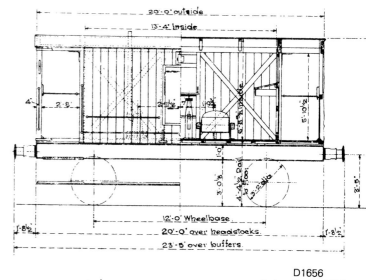

D1656
Code: BRO
Tare: 20 tons
AV brake

Figure 1

Plate 1 illustrates No. 2045 as running in c1936 in what was its original livery.

Photograph G. Y. Hemingway

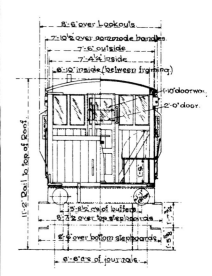

Plate 1

Plate 2 illustrates No. M277 at the end of its life when photographed at Earlestown in 1964. The livery is BR and was probably bauxite in colour. No pictures are known to the author for this type in post-1936 LMS livery.

Photograph Author's Collection

Plate 2

D1799 40 TON GOODS BRAKE VAN

Reclassified by BR as 40 Ton Freight Brake Van

Drawing No. 11/219 & 11/220 **Figure 2**

The three vehicles numbered 284723 — 25 were built at Newton Heath in 1930 to lot 549 and were the heaviest brake vans built by the LMS. They each replaced two LNWR vehicles on the Copley Hill to Armley line and spent their entire life on this service. Note the sanding gear; this was not normal practice on LMS goods brakes of standard design.

Plate 3 This illustrates No. 284723 in original condition.
Photograph British Rail

Diagram Book Page 1A

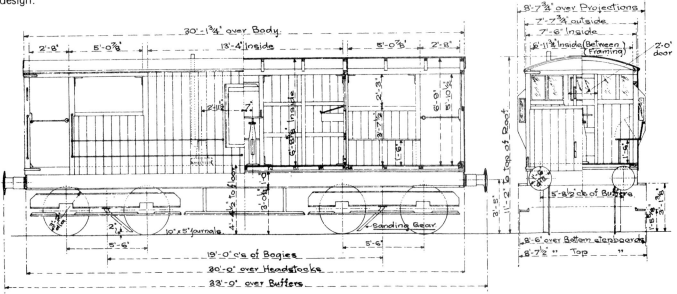

Figure 2

Plate 4

Plate 5

Plates 4 and **5** Two views of M284725 at Derby after withdrawal from service and awaiting scrapping in 1966, which indicates an active life of about 35 years.

Photograph Author's Collection

D1657 20 TON GOODS BRAKE VAN   Diagram Book Page 2

Reclassified by BR as 20 Ton Freight Brake Van

Drawing Nos. 6635 and 13/1082   **Figure 3**

Built to Lot Numbers Part 300/309. Total Lot Numbers 316/372/374/453/503/540/541.

Unlike the similar vehicles to D1656, these brake vans, which were not fitted with automatic vacuum brakes, depicted a change of 'end construction' and were flush planked — compare with **Plate 1**, diagram book page 1.

950 vehicles were built between 1927 and 1931 and some block numbers were employed: 357701-10, 357712—357884,

357886—357950; plus the following recorded random numbers: 284816, 284943, 284990, 284992, 287329, 287834, 291834, 293625, 294075, 294267, 295520, 295657, 296257, 296602/3, 318599, 318643, 319173, 319463, 319665, 320334, 325063, 326166, 328337, 329039, 329374, 357611, 357727.

It is interesting to note that two separate drawing numbers appear in the official records which also suggest that the final 50 vehicles constructed were also equipped with automatic vacuum brake through pipes. However, a number of vans may have been fitted with vacuum brakes after the original construction and photographs in BR livery of vehicles with brake pipes include Nos. M287329, M291385 and M293625. A number of plates have been selected to illustrate these vehicles.

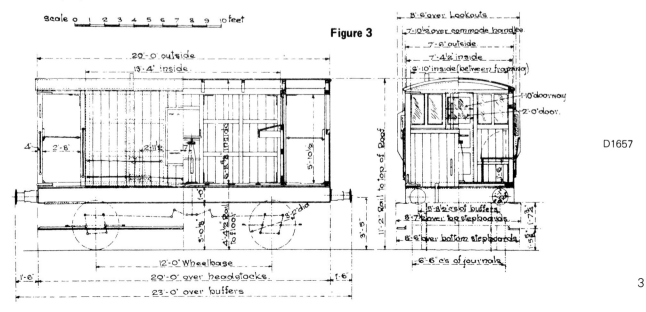

Figure 3

D1657

Plate 6 illustrates No. 357914 in original condition and is an example of lot 316 which was built at Derby in 1927/8.
Photograph British Rail

Plate 6

Plate 7 illustrates No. 357845 in service and is a most interesting picture. The end verandah and general style is consistent with D1657 but there are no side lookouts. However, the arrangement of the handrails suggests that it was intended to fit side look-outs, but it is not known how many vehicles were so equipped. It is also worth noting that in this particular photograph there appears to be no black background to the number panel. While uncommon, this practice was not unknown.
Photograph British Rail

Plate 7

4

Plate 8

Plate 8 shows M328337 which, when photographed in 1964, was carrying a Derby 1931 building plate. Note the extra strapping which apparently was fitted from very late LMS or the early BR period; this application, though widespread, was not universal.

Photograph Author's Collection

Plate 9 This picture has been selected to illustrate an example in departmental service. DM295657 was photographed at Hitchin in 1965 when allocated to the District Engineer, Kings Cross.

Photograph Author's Collection

Plate 9

5

Plate 10

D1890 20 TON GOODS BRAKE VAN

Reclassified by BR as 20 Ton Freight Brake Van

Drawing No. 12/239A   **Figure 4**

Built to Lot Numbers 715/716/757.

Introduced in 1933, this diagram heralded the beginning of the longer goods brake vans, and these 150 vans were distinguished by the extra length being added to the ends, rather than being lengthened along the van body side in the style of the more numerous and later vehicles to D1919 and D2036/2068.

Construction was all at Derby in 1933/4 with the final 50 equipped with automatic vacuum through pipes. Random numbers were allocated and the following have been recorded: 286163, 294346, 294350, 295083, 295443, 295661, 295721, 296163, 296312, 296412, 296406, 296622, 297699, 296708, with 296406 as the only piped example — see **Plate 14**.

Diagram Book Page 2A

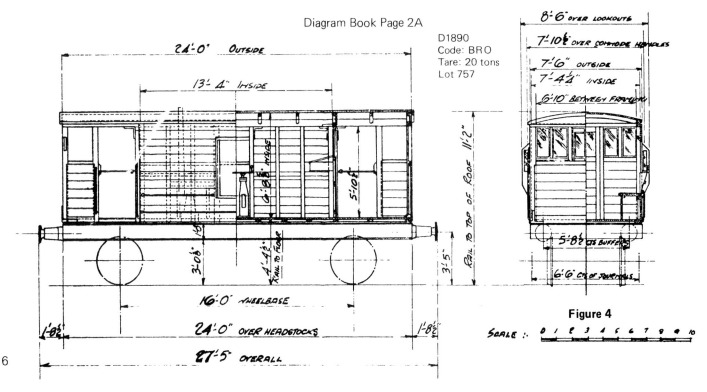

D1890
Code: BR O
Tare: 20 tons
Lot 757

Figure 4

SCALE :   0 1 2 3 4 5 6 7 8 9 10

6

◀ **Plate 10** illustrates No. 294350 in original condition and it is presumed that all were so finished.

Photograph British Rail

Plate 11

Plates **11** and **12** illustrate No. DM295721 at Hitchin in 1964, when in departmental service, while **Plate 13** illustrates No. M296412 at Kettering in 1965, after with-drawal. This photograph has been selected to illustrate the extra strapping fixed to the bodyside in the form of a vee — a common feature in the BR period on these vehicles but, as with the D1657 vehicles, not universal in its application.

Photographs Author's Collection

Finally, **Plate 14** illustrates No 296406 at Westbury in 1964. This picture has been selected to show a piped vehicle, plus a replacement side lookout, which is wider than that originally fitted.

Photograph C. M. Strevens

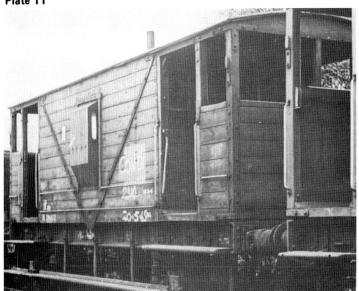

Plate 13

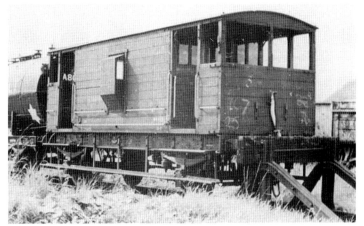

Plate 14

D1919 20 TON GOODS BRAKE VAN

Reclassified by BR as 20 Ton Freight Brake Van

Drawing No. 12/278   Lot 835) Body   **Figure 5**
             12/278C   Lot 919)

             13/2097   Lot 835) U/frame
             14/2796   Lot 919)

Built to lot numbers 835/919/1007/1103/1104.

670 vehicles were built at Derby between 1935/8 and marked the introduction of the final style of goods brake van to be used by the LMS. Apart from spanning a change of livery style, these vehicles were noteworthy inasmuch as they lacked the deeper weights to be found on vans to the later diagrams.

Running Nos. were 730000–89 piped, 730090–730669 recorded as handbrake only.

All the piped vehicles were turned out in grey and the livery change from grey to bauxite was probably around No. 730209. A picture exists which illustrates No. 730097 as a piped van identical to No. 730026 **(Plate 15)** so it is not possible to say exactly how many were so equipped when first built. Some vehicles that were originally piped were later altered to handbrake only.

This second style of longer van marked the change of design away from the style of D1890 with the half height sides attached to the van body instead of the ends, which themselves were of steel plate construction, rather than the wood of earlier designs.

Diagram Book Page 2B

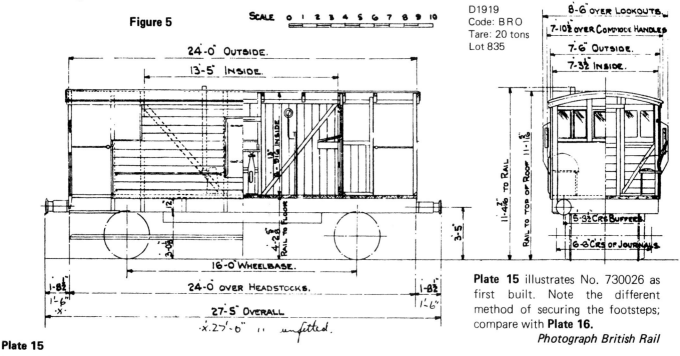

Figure 5

SCALE 0 1 2 3 4 5 6 7 8 9 10

D1919
Code: B R O
Tare: 20 tons
Lot 835

Plate 15 illustrates No. 730026 as first built. Note the different method of securing the footsteps; compare with **Plate 16**.

Photograph British Rail

Plate 15

Plate 16 shows No. 730386 in bauxite body colour, with the post-1936 style of numbering. Compare buffers on non-piped vans, with piped vehicles; see **Plate 15**.

Photograph British Rail

Plate 16

Plate 17

Plate 17 This illustrates No. M730020 of lot 835, at the end of its days at Lostock Hall in 1968. This van no longer has the through pipe with which it was originally equipped and, like **Plate 18** displays the final BR livery style.

Photograph D. P. Rowland

Plate 18

Plate 18 This features No. M730204 of lot 919 and, in view of the existence of the photograph of 730097, it does suggest that, up to No. 730209, all these vehicles were piped but, as previously mentioned, this was not officially recorded. One would expect all these first 210 vehicles to be completed as **Plate 15** and repaints into bauxite would be possibly delayed until after 1945. Photographed at Millerhill in 1964.

Photograph D. P. Rowland

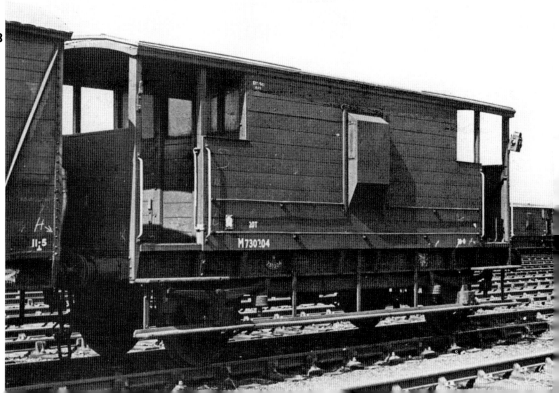

Plate 19

Plate 19 illustrates No. 295516 in original ex-works condition.

Photograph British Rail

D1940 20 TON GOODS BRAKE VAN

Diagram Book Page 2C

Reclassified by BR as 20 Ton Freight Brake Van

Drawing No. 12/217

Figure 6

100 vehicles were built to this diagram in 1933/4 to one lot, 671, and, while they retained the 20 foot length of the earlier vehicles, the wheelbase was increased in length from 12′ 0″ to 14′ 0″, probably in an attempt to provide a steadier ride at higher speeds. Without doubt, this was only an interim move in that D1890 appeared in the same year and these are illustrated on diagram book page 2A.

Random numbers were employed and the following have been recorded: 297384, 295516, 297435.

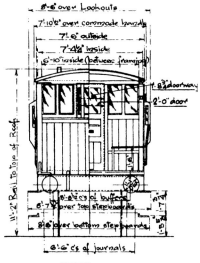

D1940
Code: BRO
Tare: 20 tons

Plate 20 illustrates No. 297384 following its withdrawal in 1964. Note the vee strapping which was added to this vehicle and probably others during BR days. The livery of these brake vans followed normal practice when carrying post-1936 bauxite livery; see **Plate 16.**

Photograph Author's Collection

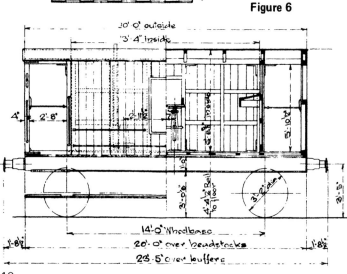

Figure 6

Plate 20

D2036 20 TON GOODS BRAKE VAN

Reclassified by BR as 20 Ton Freight Brake Van

Drawing No. 12/278 **Figure 7**

Built to lot numbers 1204/1205/1278/1279/1281/ 1291.

522 vehicles were built during the period 1940/1 carrying running Nos. 730670–731191 and were all finished in bauxite livery. It will be noted that D2036 and D1919 both enjoy the same drawing number for the body and the lot book does not specify an underframe drawing for page 2D. However, D2036 were 6" wider over the duckets when compared with D1919.

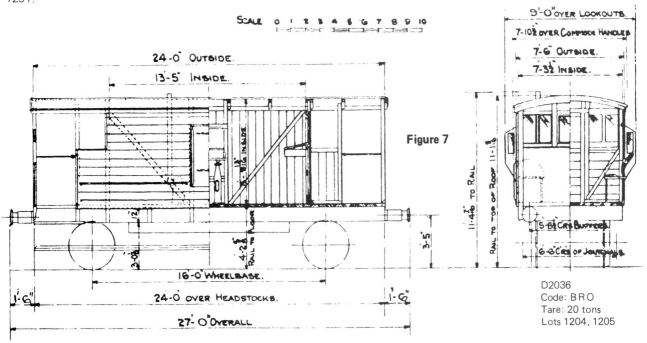

Figure 7

D2036
Code: BRO
Tare: 20 tons
Lots 1204, 1205

Plate 21 illustrates No. 730670 as built and we have a slight mystery. The date on the solebar reads 16.5.39 whereas the date of ordering in the lot book is 1940! Even if there was an error in the numbering this brake van has the wider duckets so the author is unable to provide a clear explanation for this mystery.

Photograph British Rail

Plate 22 shows No. M730836 at Millerhill in 1964. The vehicle is in light grey livery with the numbers, weights, etc. on black patches.

Photograph D. P. Rowland

Plate 23 This interior view of No. 730670 has been included to illustrate the interior layout of these vans which provided a very comfortable ride when compared with certain other goods brake vans in which the author has ridden.

Photograph British Rail

Plate 23

Plate 24 depicts No. 731885 as built in 1944.

Photograph British Rail

There was no hard and fast rule regarding the position of the lettering around the hand rail, which could either take the form of

LMS		LMS
20T	or	20T
123456		123456

If the former style was used, the 'LMS' would be placed where '20T' is on No. 731885 with the number dropped down by one plank in order to accommodate the '20T'.

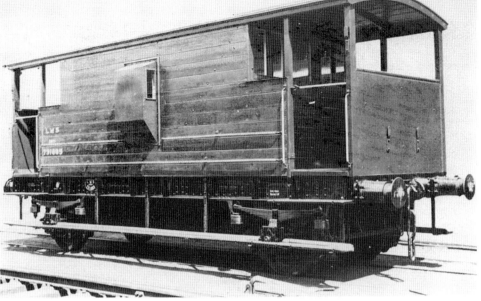

D2068 20 TON GOODS BRAKE VAN

Reclassified by BR as 20 Ton Freight Brake Van   **Figure 8**

Most lots to Drawing No. 12/278 and 13/3453
except
Lot 1471 and Lot 1517 (fitted) to 13/3790 and 12/717A
and
Lot No. 1470/1518 to 13/3789 and 12/717A

Built to lots 1316/1332/1343/1363/1387/1424/1470/ 1471/1517/1518.

Diagram 2068 was the final style of LMS goods brake van design and a large number were built between 1949/50 with the final examples entering service with the 'M' prefix under British Railways ownership. Running numbers were 731192–731741, 731746–732086, 732096–732311, 732321-732545. Of these, 732396–732470 were fitted with automatic vacuum brakes, the remainder were 'hand brake only'.

The body design appears to be very similar to D2036 but the underframe carried much deeper weights, which went down behind the footsteps. Compare **Plate 24** (D2068) with **Plate 21** (D2036).

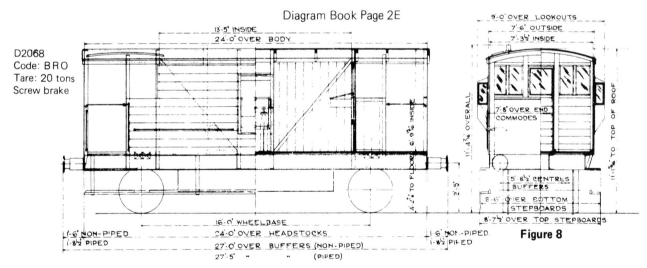

Diagram Book Page 2E

D2068
Code: B R O
Tare: 20 tons
Screw brake

Figure 8

Plate 25

Plate 25 depicts No. M732396 built in 1948 by British Railways and is an example of a vehicle with automatic vacuum brake. Note the longer buffers made possible by including a packing piece.

Photograph British Rail

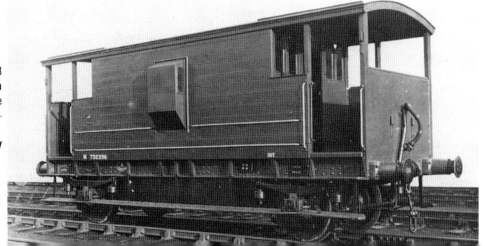

D2096 BRAKE VAN, FREIGHT

Drawing No. 12/678   **Figure 9**

The Lot Book records four 20-ton goods brakes built in 1943 to lot 1352 at Wolverton and the LMS allocated numbers 731742–5, but one went to each of the four British companies and they carried LMS 731742 tare 21.6.2, LNER 760948 tare 20.6.2., GWR 35927 tare 20.10.2, SR 56060 tare 20.11.2. They were built to RCH standards and the design appeared to be based upon LNER practice as this 'LMS' design carried sand boxes, which were not an LMS feature. Nevertheless, the basic dimensions were LMS, although the ducket width of 8' 9'' was 3'' less than current LMS practice. No pictures are known to exist of the other three vehicles and **Plate 26** illustrating No. 731742 shows its original condition.

Photograph British Rail

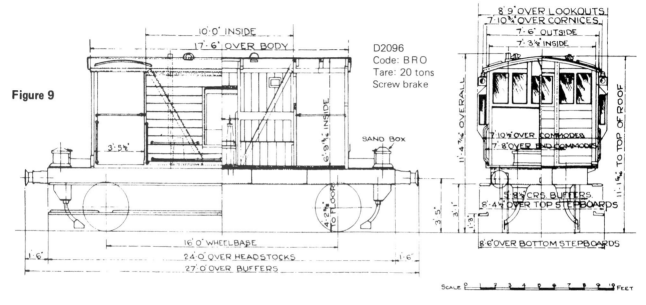

Figure 9

D2096
Code: B R O
Tare: 20 tons
Screw brake

Plate 26

Plate 27

D2148 20 TON GOODS BRAKE VAN WAPPING TUNNEL WORKING

Diagram Book Page 2G

Drawing No. 11/532 and 13/3987 **Figure 10**

9 vehicles were built in 1948 to lot 1498 and were numbered M732312–732320. They were built for working through Wapping Tunnel and, like the vans described on page 2H, had a vestibule at one end with steel bar gates instead of the steel bar at the access opening and the same kind of screw brake arrangement. Fortunately, two pictures of M732317 exist and these are depicted in **Plates 27** and **28** showing the branding and 'Return to Liverpool, Edge Hill'. Other points worthy of note are side lamp brackets at one end only and only one tail lamp bracket.

Photograph British Rail

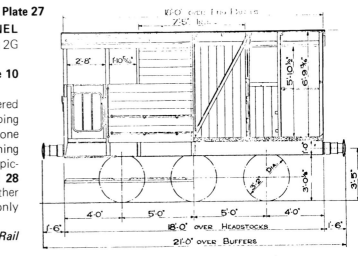

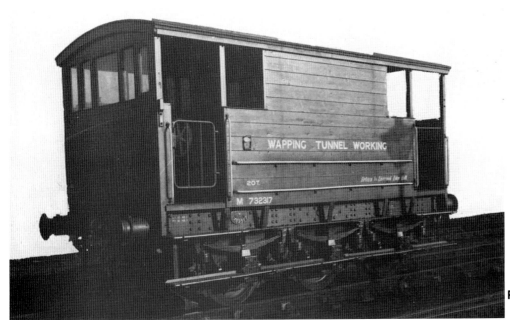

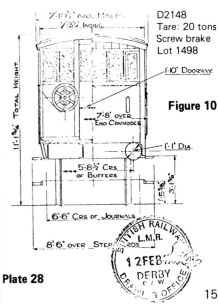

D2148
Tare: 20 tons
Screw brake
Lot 1498

Figure 10

Plate 28

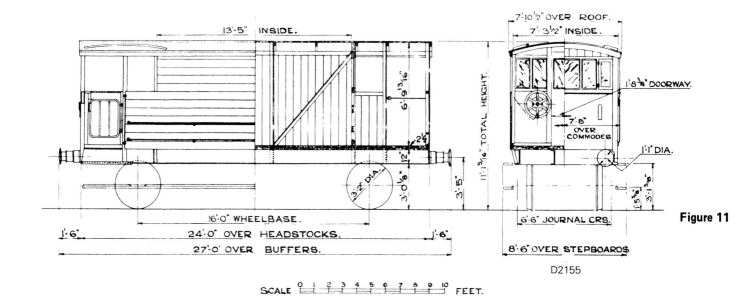

13'-5" INSIDE.

6'-9 3/16"

7'-10 1/2" OVER ROOF.
7'-3 1/2" INSIDE.

1'-8 3/4" DOORWAY.

7'-8" OVER COMMODES

1'-1" DIA.

11'-1 5/16" TOTAL HEIGHT

3'-5"

3'-0 1/16"

2 1/4"

12"

3'-2" DIA.

6'-6" JOURNAL CRS.

8'-6" OVER STEPBOARDS

Figure 11

D2155

16'-0" WHEELBASE.
24'-0" OVER HEADSTOCKS.
27'-0" OVER BUFFERS.

1'-6"

1'-6"

SCALE 0 1 2 3 4 5 6 7 8 9 10 FEET.

D2155 20 TON GOODS BRAKE VAN   Diagram Book Page 2H

Drawing No. 11/489 and 13/3662   **Figure 11**

The 9 vehicles built to lot 1411 in 1947 and numbered 732087–732095 were unlike any previous construction. The verandah was glazed at one end only and side duckets were not fitted. The ends, which became vestibules, had steel gates across the access openings instead of the more usual safety bar. Unlike all other goods brake vans which had vertical brake columns mounted within the body, these 9 had hand brake wheels horizontally on the ends of the body, long shafts were attached to them and worked through bevel gears to a vertically mounted screw within the body. It is not known for certain just for what special traffic they were built and, no pictures are known to the author.

D1659 20 TON GOODS BRAKE VAN   Diagram Book Page 4

Reclassified by BR as 20 Ton Freight Brake Van

Drawing No. 5944   **Figure 12**

Built to lot numbers 37/114/Part 119/136/199/200/201/241/Part 300 and Part 309.

Although page 4 in the LMS book, these vehicles, built between 1924 and 1927 were constructed to the final Midland Railway design, using a Midland Railway drawing and a total of 849 vans were allocated to the diagram. Some block numbers were used: 357401–357700; plus the following recorded random numbers: 402/416, 134900, 144182, 280663, 281304, 357240, 357487, 357498, 357611 and 357885. All were hand brake only. Vans fitted with automatic vacuum brakes were built and, although page 3 was allocated to D1658, all these vehicles were built to Midland Railway lots and so fall outside the scope of this volume, but are recorded in Chapter 11 of *An Illustrated History of Midland Wagons, Volume Two,* published by OPC.

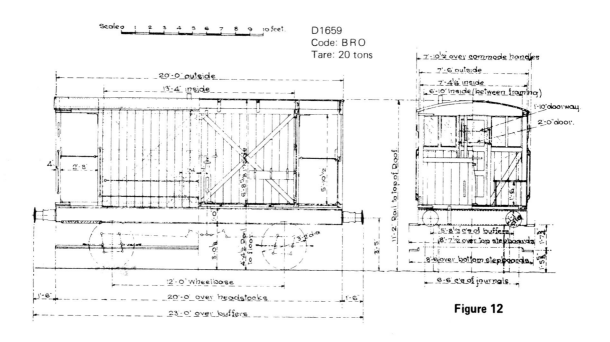

Scale 0 1 2 3 4 5 6 7 8 9 10 feet.

D1659
Code: BRO
Tare: 20 tons

20'-0" outside
13'-4" inside

7'-10 1/2" over commode handles
7'-6" outside
7'-4 1/4" inside
6'-10" inside (between framing)

1'-10" doorway
2'-0" door.

11'-2" Rail to top of Roof.

5'-8 1/2" c's of buffers.
8'-7 1/2" over top stepboards.
8'-6" over bottom stepboards.

6'-6" c's of journals.

12'-0" wheelbase
20'-0" over headstocks
23'-0" over buffers

3'-5"

Figure 12

16

As seen in **Plate 29** the Midland tablet racks were fitted and it is believed that all vehicles were so equipped when built. In due course these racks were removed — see **Plate 30**. As befits Midland practice, no side duckets were fitted.

Plate 30

Plate 29

Plate 30 illustrates No. 280663 in post-1936 bauxite livery. Pictures of brake vans in this livery style are rather rare and this style should be used by modellers who wish to depict D1656/7/9 in post-1936 livery condition.

Photograph Author's Collection

Plate 31

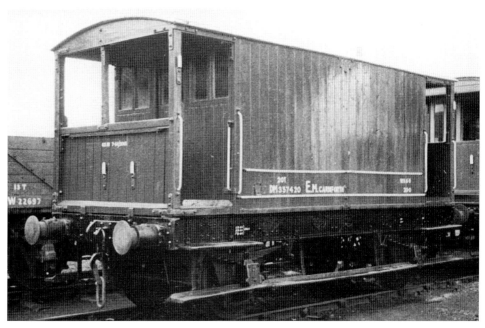

Plate 31 illustrates a vehicle in departmental service. No. DM357420 was allocated to Carnforth in 1964 and, when photographed, it was painted green.

Photograph Author's Collection

NO DIAGRAM, 20T GOODS BRAKE VAN

Before moving on to consider plough brake vans, the opportunity has been taken to illustrate goods brake van No. 281304 in original and BR ownership (**Plates 32** and **33**).

The exact history of the vehicle is not known but it is believed to have been part of lot 241 built at Derby in 1926 and was obviously experimental. No doubt it was classified as Diagram 1656 but was provided with an all steel body.

Plate 32 — *Photograph British Rail*

Plate 34 shows plough brake van No. 197263 with a ▶ hopper ballast wagon No. 197273 and the ploughs can be clearly seen, with the nearest lowered and the far one raised.

Photograph British Rail

Plate 33 — *Photograph Author's Collection*

Plate 33

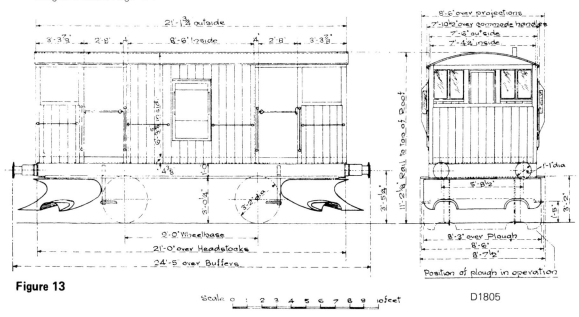

Figure 13

Scale 0 1 2 3 4 5 6 7 8 9 10 feet

D1805

D1805 PLOUGH BRAKE VAN

Drawing No. 12/202　　　　　　　　**Figure 13**

In 1932, 9 vehicles were built to lot 635 — the underframes by Cravens and the bodies at Derby — with allocated running numbers 197263–197271. Plough brake vans were used with Engineers' trains and were sometimes described as ballast brake vans. They were equipped with a plough at each end which, when lowered, would spread the ballast dropped from the hopper wagon; see **Plate 35.**

The lot book records two plough vans built to lot 372 but it is not known for certain just what these two vehicles were. The photographs used with pages 4A and 4B are the only ones known to the author and it would seem that they were painted red oxide rather than freight stock grey.

Plate 34

Plate 35 This posed photograph shows van No. 197269 being used in conjunction with an ex-CR 15 ton brake van No. 353355 and a train of hopper wagons. It will be noted that the plough can be seen spreading the ballast.

Photograph British Rail

Plate 36 Both ploughs are raised on this picture of No. 197263. Note the 9' 0" WB. No doubt speeds were low; these vans would not have given a comfortable ride otherwise.

Photograph British Rail

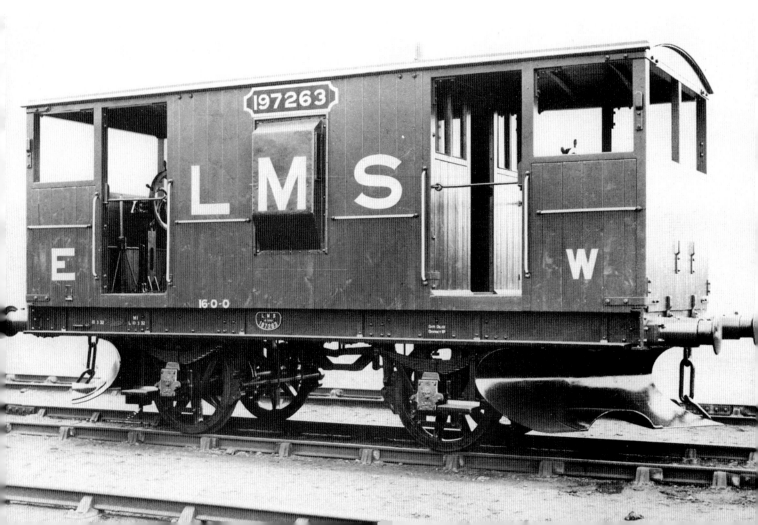

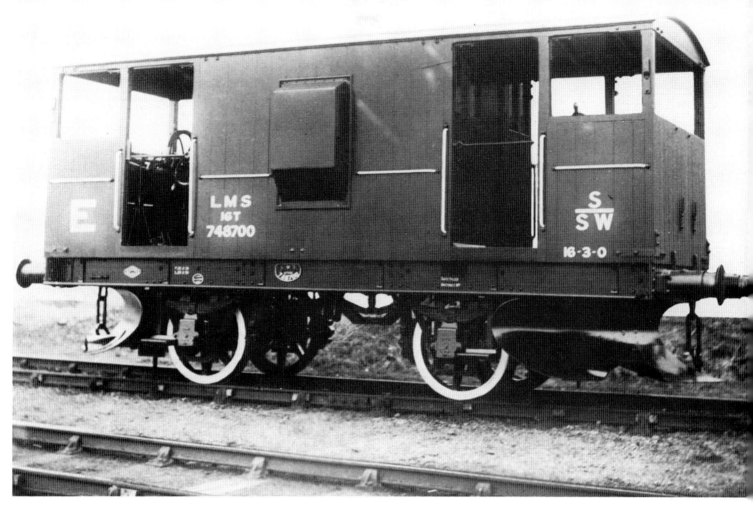

D2025 PLOUGH BRAKE VAN

Drawing No. 12/202A   **Figure 14**

One vehicle only No. 748700, was built by Pickering in 1939 to lot 1161 and the only difference was an extra 6" over the lookout. It will be noted that, unlike the earlier vehicles, No. 748700 carried post-1936 livery style, and was allocated to Scotland, South West.

Plate 37 illustrates this van as completed by Pickerings.
Photograph British Rail

Diagram Book Page 4B

Scale 0 1 2 3 4 5 6 7 8 9 10 feet

Figure 14

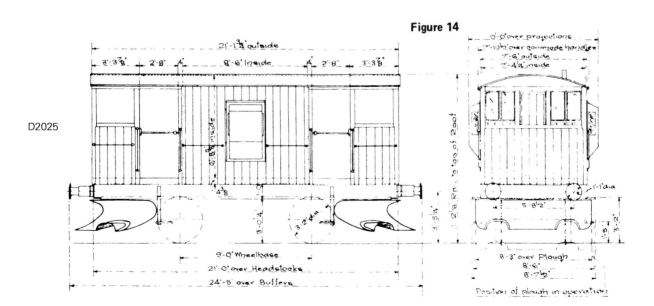

D1660 BANANA VAN

Drawing No. 6162 Lots 204/6/222   **Figure 15**
        6408 Lot 239/307/452/495/6

400 vans were built to drawing 6162 during 1925/6 and 600 vans to drawing No. 6408 between 1926 and 1930. The available evidence suggests that the vans built to drawing 6162 were not originally built with the extra strapping on the body sides as shown on **Plate 39.**

Banana vans were built with double-skinned bodies. To assist the ripening process, steam heating coils were provided in the roof space and steam was passed through heating pipe connections from the train engine. During World War II, the import of bananas in to the UK ceased and these vans were used for other traffic. Random numbers were used and the following are recorded: running numbers to drawing No. 6162 — 14284, 28862, running numbers to drawing No. 6408 — 7888, 212740, 265063, 268504. Three photographs have been selected to illustrate these vehicles.

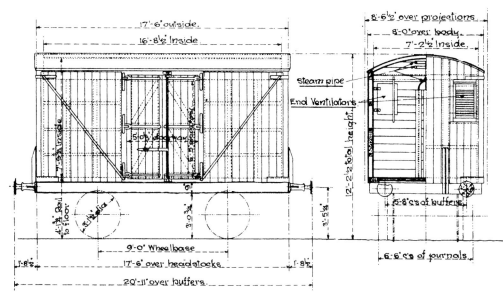

D1660
Code: BNV
Tare: 8 tons 17 cwt 2 qrs
Carrying capacity: 10 tons
Fully fitted and steam heated
Doors each side
'Morton' brake

Figure 15

Plate 38 shows van No. 28862 when first built to drawing 6162.
Photograph British Rail

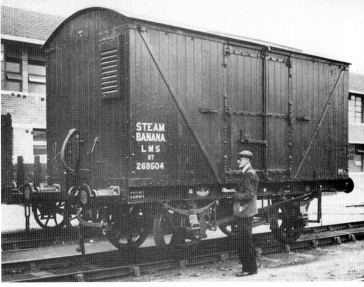

Plate 39 Banana van No. 265063 appears to be similar to the vehicle depicted in **Plate 38** but careful inspection will reveal the 'N' 'non common user' branding at each end plus the extra strapping used on vehicles built to drawing No. 6408. A photograph not used in this work was taken c1934 and shows van No. 212740 with a 12" high 'X' on the right hand door and a Fyffes sign approximately 12" square was located at the left hand end of the van about two-thirds up the side.

Photograph British Rail

Plate 40 This picture was taken in October1945 and is interesting in that it shows the signwriter having just completed the lettering of a vehicle which had been returned to banana traffic after the end of World War II. Therefore between these three plates, we are able to show pre-war grey and post-war bauxite. Under British Railways ownership the word 'steam' seems to have been discontinued and the number was prefixed with a letter 'M'.

Photograph British Rail

D2111 BANANA VAN

Diagram Book Page 5A

Drawing No. 13/3711
      13/3707

Figure 16

100 vehicles were built in 1946 to lot 1421 and the allocated running numbers were 570000—570099. It is interesting to note that they were built on a 9' 0" wheelbase and, unlike the earlier construction to D1660, these 100 had a prominent casing over the steam heating pipe at each end.

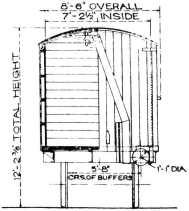

Figure 16

D2111
Code: B N V
Tare: 9 tons 2 cwt
Carrying capacity: 10 tons
Fully fitted and steam heated
'Morton' brake

Plate 41 illustrates van No. 570007 when first constructed. One other picture showing them in British Railways livery indicates that at least one vehicle, No. 570075, ran with open spoke wheels.

Photograph British Rail

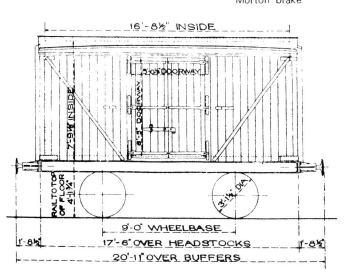

Plate 42 illustrates No. 12098 as originally built.

Photograph British Rail

Plate 44 shows a 'trade' built ▶ vehicle No. 292722, built by the Metropolitan, Carriage & Wagon Finance Co. in original condition. This plate is interesting in that it shows a piped vehicle, a full length rainstrip (not visible on No. 12098 or, indeed, on any LMS-built vehicles) and yet a third arrangement of the drop door.

Photograph HMRS Collection

Plate 42

D1661 CATTLE WAGON   Diagram Book Page 6

Drawing No. 5540 up to lot 286   **Figure 17**
Drawing No. 13/1042 from lot 310 to lot 539

Built to lot numbers Midland lot 987, LMS lots 3/106/ 142/152/193/238/310/329/368/437/501/538/539.

The earliest vehicles produced to this diagram were a Midland lot No. 987 for 300 vehicles ordered in 1922 and actually built the following year. The lot contained 136 with through pipes and 164 with hand brake only. These 300 were followed by a further 4138 vehicles up to 1932, whereupon future construction was to D1840. The use of two drawings, coupled with the fact that construction was at Derby, Newton Heath and 'the trade', explains why there are small variations which generally centre around the depth of the drop doors and this will be seen in the plates selected to illustrate these vehicles. In later years, the decline in rail-carried cattle traffic led to some vehicles being branded for 'Ale Traffic'. Known running numbers: 1621, 8521, 12098, 14400, 69453, 214875, 230909, 265032, 267352, 292372 (piped), 292722 (piped), 296362 (piped), 301591 (piped), 302351 (piped), 325137 (branded 'Ale').

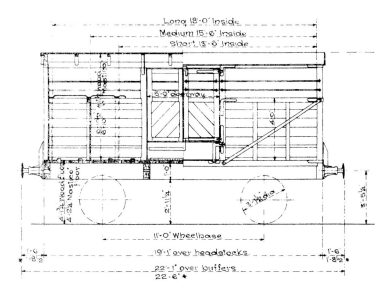

Figure 17

D1661
Codes, hand brake only: C
          hand brake and through pipe: PC
Tares, hand brake and through pipe
          plain wood floor: 7 tons 14 cwt
          1 qr
          hand brake only and 'Mastico'
          floor: 8 tons 2 cwt 2qrs
          hand brake and through pipe,
          'Mastico' floor: 8 tons 6 cwt
Carrying capacity: 12 tons
Independent brake on each side of wagon.
Dimensions marked thus * only for wagons fitted with through pipe.

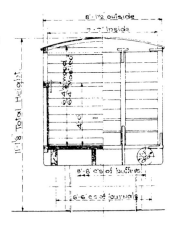

Plate 43 illustrates No.230909, and attention is drawn to the difference in the drop door, when compared with **Plate 42**.

Photograph G. Y. Hemingway

Plate 43

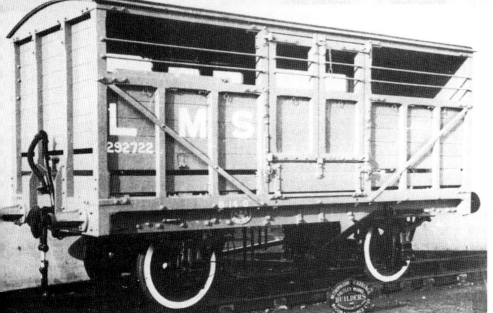

Plate 44

Plate 45 This row of new cattle wagons, just about to leave Charles Roberts, is interesting and the white tyres to the wheels may have been painted for photographic purposes. A quantity were built by 'the trade' in 1925/6 and it can be clearly seen that these are fitted with automatic vacuum brake through pipes. The running number of the first wagon appears to be No. 292372 and the next vehicle seems to be 2923?? so it would seem this batch may have been numbered in the 2923XX series.

Photograph Charles Roberts
Courtesy National Railway Museum

Plate 45

Plate 46

Plate 46 No. 265032 was built in September 1926 and this picture has been used to draw attention to the ironwork variations whereby a stout plate at both ends is used, a feature found also on D1840 (Page 6D) vehicles; identically constructed wagons were numbered 267332 and 69453.

Photograph British Rail

Plates **47** and **48** are of No. 214875 in bauxite livery, C1937.
Photographs Ross Pochin

Plate 47

Plate 48

Plate 49

Plate 49 This picture illustrates cattle wagon No. M14400 in 1962. Note the traces of 'LMS' above the '12T'; almost certainly this vehicle was repainted in LMS bauxite livery. It is interesting to see that the vehicle is carrying its 12 ton capacity, painted onto the bodyside. Note also the absence of a rainstrip but cross-strips over the roof are just visible on the original print.
Photograph D. P. Rowland

D1818 CONVERTIBLE SHEEP AND CATTLE WAGON

No drawing number known

Figure 18

One only was built in 1929 by G. R. Turner to lot 459 and, unfortunately the lot book does not give a drawing reference. One of the only photographs known to exist came to light after this work was completed and has been reproduced on page v.

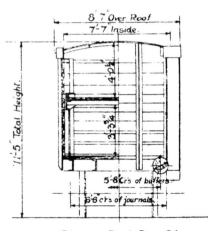

Diagram Book Page 6A

D1818

Figure 18

Code: None allocated
Tare: 8 tons 18 cwt
Carrying capacity: 12 tons
Fitted with through vacuum pipe
Independent brake on each side of wagon
Clearance for cattle with upper floor raised: 6'0"
Lot 459

D1824 DOUBLE DECK SHEEP TRUCK

D1824
Code: None allocated
Tare: 9 tons 1 cwt 2 qrs
Carrying capacity: 12 tons
Fitted with AVB through pipe
Independent brake on each side of wagon
Headroom for cattle : 6'4½''
Headroom for sheep : 3'3'' bottom deck
Headroom for sheep : 3'1½'' top deck
Lot 520

Drawing No. 13/1321   **Figure 19**

A single vehicle, built at Derby to lot 520 in 1930, was allocated to this diagram and no further information is available. Similar vehicles existed on the Highland Railway and it is most likely that D1824 originally went to that part of the LMS system.

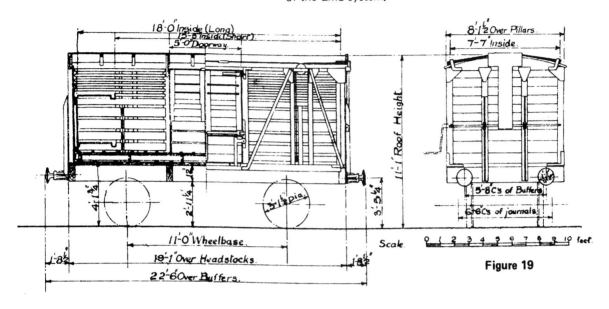

Figure 19

D1819 CALF VAN

Drawing No. 13/1275   **Figure 20**

10 vehicles were built at Derby in 1929 to lot 473 and were, in effect, LMS versions of an old Midland Railway design. Very few pictures exist and the only confirmed running numbers are 327897 **(Plate 50)** and 327099. Both pictures being taken during the British Railways period of ownership when branded for use as fruit vans. Note that M327897 is not vacuum fitted, the hose is merely part of a 'through pipe system' and that the pipe is painted a lighter colour than the BR grey used on the body.

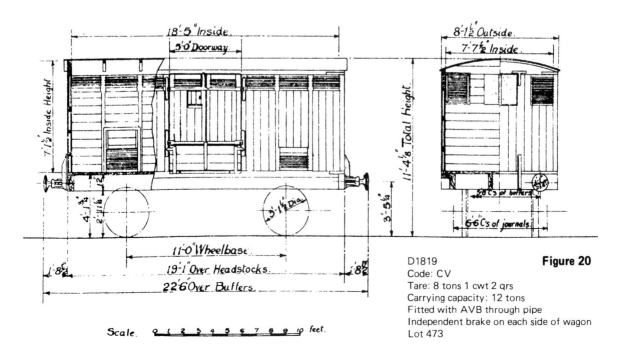

D1819
Code: CV
Tare: 8 tons 1 cwt 2 qrs
Carrying capacity: 12 tons
Fitted with AVB through pipe
Independent brake on each side of wagon
Lot 473

Figure 20

Plates **50** and **50A** were both taken at Axminster on 20th April, 1961.

Photograph A. E. West

D1840 CATTLE WAGON

Diagram Book Page 6D

Drawing No. 13/1736   Lot 652/653
Drawing No. 13/1900A   Lot 711/712/756

Figure 21

Built to lot numbers 652/653/711/712/756.

To all intents and purposes, these vehicles were identical to D1661, apart from the drop door variations and the fact that all of the lots comprising D1840 were fitted with A.V. hand brakes of Morton pattern and steam heating pipes and were not equipped with the double side brakes of D1661.

Running numbers 81078, 239381, 266640, 267002, 267332, 292052 and 293612.

Plate 52 is a wartime picture and it shows (reading from right to left) Midlan Railway cattle wagon No. 14540 in pre-1936 LMS grey livery, No. 292052 o D1840 also in post-1936 bauxite livery. The numbers of the other three catt wagons appear to be 111078, 29274? and LNER No. 417007.

Photograph British Ra

Plate 50A

D1840
Code: FC
Tare: 8 tons 11 cwt 3 qrs
Carrying capacity: 12 tons
Fitted with AV and hand brakes and
steam heating pipe
Lots 652, 653, 711, 712

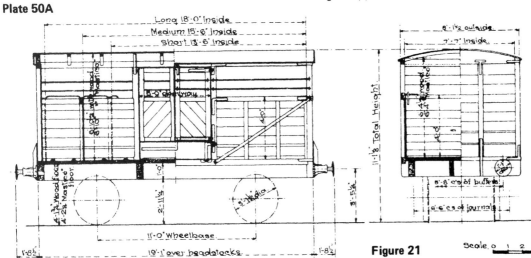

Figure 21

Plate 51

Plate 51 No. 293612 in ex-works condition with the date on the solebar reading '14.12.33'. Note the 'N' on the end of the headstock.

Photograph British Rail

Plate 52

Plate 53

Plate 53 shows a D1840 wagon in British Railways ownership. M266640 was photographed in May 1962 at Appleby and attention is drawn to the placing of the 'M' which is most unusual. Note the cross-bracing on the roof. Finally, attention is drawn to the fact that cattle wagons to both diagrams employed solid, open spoke end disc wheels.

Photograph D. Jenkinson

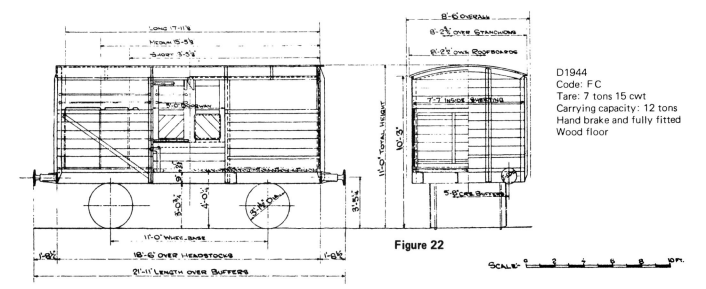

D1944
Code: F C
Tare: 7 tons 15 cwt
Carrying capacity: 12 tons
Hand brake and fully fitted
Wood floor

Figure 22

SCALE

D1944 CATTLE WAGON

Diagram Book Page 6E

Drawing No. 13/2112

Figure 22

In 1935 a final 100 cattle wagons were built by the LMS to lot 834 and these were the last livestock vehicles to be built to freight stock diagrams. Allocated to lot 834, their running numbers were 710000—710099 and all were turned out in grey livery as **Plate 54**. It is unlikely that many ever received post-1936 bauxite and probably all were liveried in BR red oxide as fitted vehicles. Regrettably, no photographs are known to exist, other than the official view **(Plate 54)** which shows the original condition.

Plate 54

Plate 54 illustrates cattle wagon 710010 in original condition as built in 1935. In due course, similar vehicles were built for British Railways after nationalization.

Photograph British Rail

Plate 56 This illustrates van No. 5803 in original condition and is a hand brake only vehicle.

Photograph British Rail

Plate 55

Plate 55 This illustrates a British Railways built vehicle No. B890048, constructed at Derby in 1950 to lot 2022. There are a number of very subtle differences to be seen, such as the angle of the end stanchions, the cornerplates at solebar level, the axleboxes, buffer bodies, spring hangers and the shape of the brake lever.

Photograph British Rail

D1663 GOODS VAN   Diagram Book Page 8

Drawing No. 5645   **Figure 23**

Built to lot numbers 73/186—192

850 vans were built during the period 1924/26 to this diagram and 750 were built by the trade. These vehicles were the first vans to be built with steel ends and, as will be noted from the diagram, this batch was not ventilated. During the 'grey body' livery period fully fitted vehicles carried a large white 'X' positioned centrally on the bottom half of the door; see also **Plate 64** (D1814). However, when built these vans carried their running number at the left hand end, not on the door. Finally, it should be noted that fitted vans had the buffer body length increased by inserting a packing piece next to the van body.

Random running numbers included: 5803, 133592 (fitted), 148117, 151368, 155543, 156079, 158995, 180392, 182378, 186205, 197891, 200009, 232487, 271963, 283704, 291859, 297523.

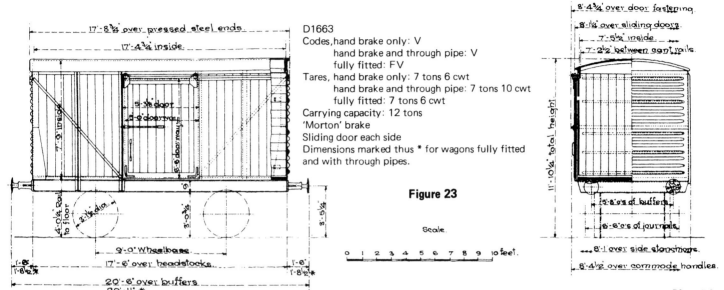

D1663
Codes, hand brake only: V
       hand brake and through pipe: V
       fully fitted: FV
Tares, hand brake only: 7 tons 6 cwt
       hand brake and through pipe: 7 tons 10 cwt
       fully fitted: 7 tons 6 cwt
Carrying capacity: 12 tons
'Morton' brake
Sliding door each side
Dimensions marked thus * for wagons fully fitted
and with through pipes.

Figure 23

Scale.

0 1 2 3 4 5 6 7 8 9 10 feet

Plate 56

Plate 57 This picture has been selected to show a vacuum brake vehicle, No. 148117, as running c1936. When compared with No. 5803, it will be noted that a small 'LMS' is on the door and this suggests that the van was repainted in the early 1930s when this style was in vogue.

Photograph G. Y. Hemingway

Plate 58 illustrates DM155543 in departmental traffic as a tool van in 1965. Readers will note that these three plates depict solid spoke, open spoke and disc wheels.

Photograph Author's Collection

D1832A GOODS VAN

Diagram Book Page 8A

Drawing No. 5645

Figure 24

Built to lot numbers 443–445/545.

3,000 vehicles were built to lots 443/4/5 at Wolverton in 1929/30 with a further 450 to lot 545 in 1930/1 using the same drawing number as D1663 but for these 3,450 vehicles a ventilated system was employed with two end ventilators and four roof vents.

Random running numbers included: 155001, 155005, 150706, 156079, 156602, 157259, 160222, 193228, 197891, 203975.

Plate 59 illustrates fitted van No. 203975 and this is the only vehicle recorded by the author as a fitted vehicle, photographed at Wolverton when built.

Photograph British Rail

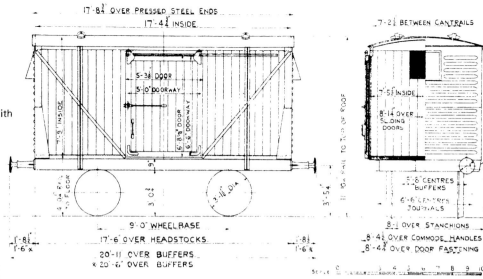

D1832A

Codes, hand brake only: V
        hand brake and through pipe: FV
Fully fitted
Tare: 7 tons 7 cwt
Carrying capacity: 12 tons
'Morton' type hand brake
Dimensions marked thus ·X· are for vehicles with hand brake only

Figure 24

Plate 60 This picture of No. 155005 should be compared with No. 203975, illustrated in **Plate 59**. Note 'Ventilated' and 'Ventilated Van' a legend later discontinued. Again, it is worth noting the use of spoked and disc wheels.

Photograph British Rail

Plate 61 This picture shows a van in bauxite livery as running in 1939. When originally built there is some evidence to suggest they were all liveried as shown in **Plates 59** and **60** but other pictures of vans in grey during the 1930s suggest that the words 'Ventilated' or 'Ventilated Van' were discontinued and the number was moved to the bottom of the door, often with '12T' above it. When repainted in the post-1936 livery, then the style adopted was as shown in the plate.

Photograph A. E. West

Plate 62 This picture shows M157259 in 1964 when condemned and at the end of its life. Note the replacement axleboxes. This picture also displays the method of lettering employed by BR during this period.

Photograph Author's Collection

Plate 61

Plate 62

D1808
Codes, hand brake only: V
       hand brake and through pipe: V
       fully fitted: FV
Tares, hand brake only: 7 tons 6 cwt
       hand brake and through pipe: 7 tons
       10 cwt
       fully fitted: 7 tons 16 cwt
Carrying capacity: 12 tons
'Morton' brake
Sliding door each side
Dimensions marked thus * for wagons fully
fitted and with through pipes.

Figure 25

D1808 GOODS VAN   Diagram Book Page 8C

Drawing No.   13/1880   **Figure 25**
            12/231

Before dealing with this diagram, it should be noted that there
was no record of a page 8B in the copy of the diagram book used
when compiling this volume.

1,100 vans were built at Wolverton to lot No. 672 and were
allocated to page 8C and the absence of block numbers makes it
rather difficult to be certain exactly which vehicles were built to
this diagram in that D1812 and D1830 were almost identical
and, as far as the running numbers are concerned, these three dia-

grams will be considered together.

Known running numbers included, 131391, 154652, 157050,
170415, 176059, 202716, 215260, 227382, 232586, 232588,
278261. Note that D1830 is page 8D and D1812 page 8F.

Therefore a selection of photographs has been chosen to
illustrate these three diagrams but only one depicts a vehicle in
LMS livery. However, it is felt that the fitted vehicles would have
been liveried as van No. 91548 in **Plate 64** and the unfitted
vehicles would not have carried the 'N' or 'X' but would otherwise have been similar.

Finally, attention is drawn to the fact that some vehicles
were, according to the diagram, equipped with wheels 3' 6½"
in diameter.

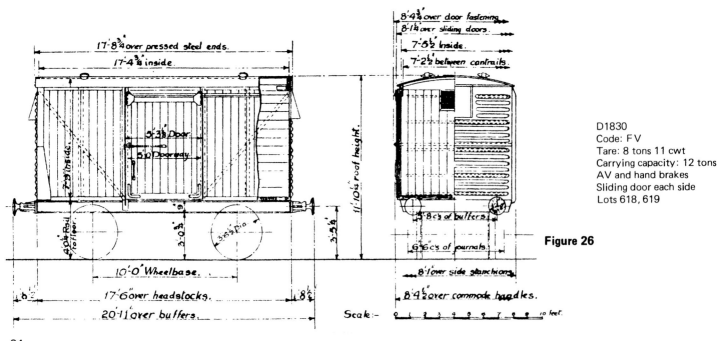

D1830
Code: FV
Tare: 8 tons 11 cwt
Carrying capacity: 12 tons
AV and hand brakes
Sliding door each side
Lots 618, 619

Figure 26

D1830 GOODS VAN   Diagram Book Page 8D

Drawing No. 13/1569   **Figure 26**

Built to lot numbers 618/619.

A total of 2,405 vehicles to this diagram were constructed in 1932/3 with 2,000 fitted with automatic vacuum brakes. See page 8C for details of running numbers.

Plate 63 (above) illustrates M131391 as running in 1965. The works plate records that it was built at Derby and the lot book states that the Derby lot of 405 were not fitted with automatic vacuum brakes, therefore the author assumes that M131391 was so equipped during the British Railways period of ownership when many vehicles were altered in this manner.

Photograph Author's Collection

D1814 GOODS VAN   Diagram Book Page 8E

Drawing No. 13/1880   **Figure 27**
            12/231

Built to lot numbers 674/675/713/714.

Readers will note that the drawing numbers are identical to D1808, yet the body style on the diagram is very different and the author is not able to give any explanation except to suggest that there was an error in the official records.

Construction of the four lots in 1933 totalled 999 — an unusual figure. Known running numbers included: 91548, 103994, 112372, 114982, 126589, 127684, 131368, 156707 (fitted), 156079, 177779, 182378, 186308, 186851, 186852, 197891, 202684, 223779, 232487, 271418, 271963, 283704.

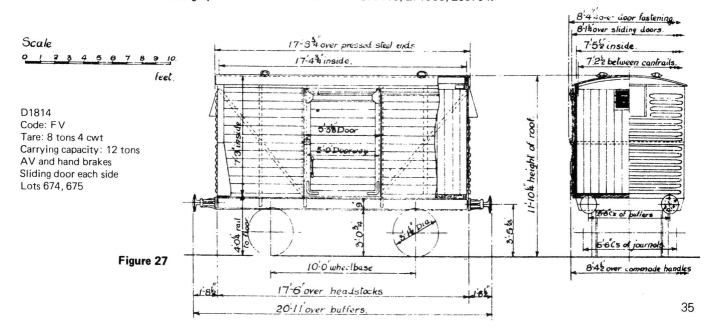

Scale
0 1 2 3 4 5 6 7 8 9 10
feet.

D1814
Code: F V
Tare: 8 tons 4 cwt
Carrying capacity: 12 tons
AV and hand brakes
Sliding door each side
Lots 674, 675

Figure 27

Plate 64

Plate 65

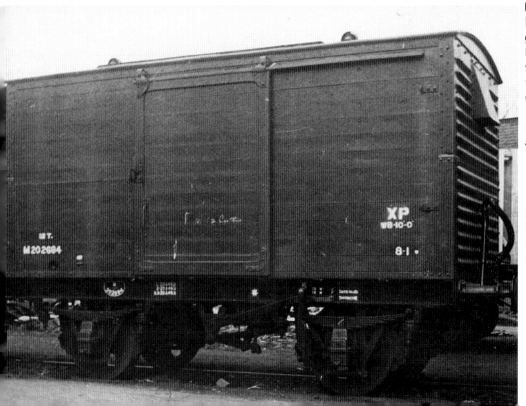

Plate **64** illustrates No. 91548 in the livery style employed by the LMS for goods van construction at the time it was built. Readers will note that, just as there was a considerable variety of goods vans, there was equally a variety of livery styles employed prior to the adoption of bauxite livery and the grouping of the running number, 'LMS' and tonnage into the bottom left hand corner.

Photograph British Rail

Plate **65** illustrates M202684 in BR bauxite livery c1949, before the use of black patches upon which the running numbers, etc. were painted.

Photograph Loco & General

Drawing No. 13/1335A   **Figure 28**
13/1396

One lot only, No. 544, for 1,050 vans built at Wolverton in 1930/1, was allocated to this diagram and, only one official picture is known to exist. Three plates have been selected to represent this page but the remarks on page 8C D1808 refer to these two pictures concerning livery.

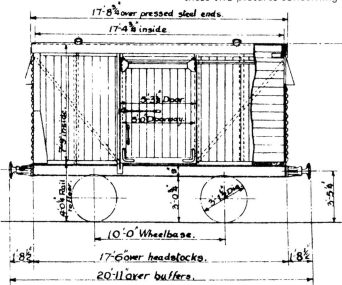

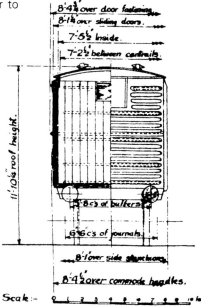

D1812
Code: PV
Tare: 8 tons 11 cwt
Carrying capacity: 12 tons
Hand brake and through pipe
Sliding door each side
Lots 544, 545

Figure 28

Plate 66

Plate **66** illustrates M146363 as running c1965 in British Railways ownership and it is interesting to note the absence of roof ventilators when compared with the diagram. In fact, pages 8C, 8D, 8E and 8F all had vans without roof ventilators, even though the diagrams suggest that they were so equipped and no explanation can be given with certainty.

Photograph Author's Collection

Plate 67

Plate **67** illustrates No. DM202716 in departmental service in 1964 after it had been fitted with steps beneath the doorway.

Photograph Author's Collection

Plate 68

Plate 68 This picture, taken at Wolverton, shows No. 232586 when first built and clearly illustrates the grey livery adopted for lot 554.

Photograph British Rail

Plate 69

Plate 69 The paint date on the solebar reads '13/3/25' and this picture illustrates van No. 335843 being lettered before entering traffic. The Wolverton built vehicles to lots 107/113 were fitted and this is an example in its original condition.

Photograph British Rail

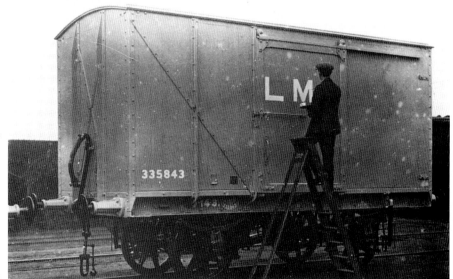

D1664 GOODS VAN   Diagram Book Page 9

Drawing No. 5669   **Figure 29**

Built to lot numbers 34/Part 36/107/113.

2,544 vans were built to this diagram at Wolverton and Derby during the period 1924/6 and the basis for the design was the final batch of covered goods wagons constructed by the Midland Railway, although the Midland vehicles had a longer wheelbase than the first of these new standard LMS vans.

Known running numbers included: 213780, 236466, 263141, 291859, 295601, 305207, 335843, 344226.

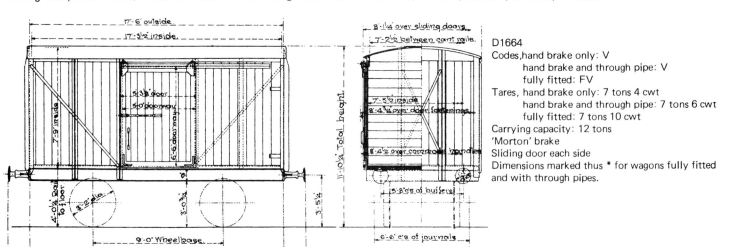

D1664
Codes, hand brake only: V
     hand brake and through pipe: V
     fully fitted: FV
Tares, hand brake only: 7 tons 4 cwt
     hand brake and through pipe: 7 tons 6 cwt
     fully fitted: 7 tons 10 cwt
Carrying capacity: 12 tons
'Morton' brake
Sliding door each side
Dimensions marked thus * for wagons fully fitted and with through pipes.

Figure 29

Plate 70 This illustrates No. 309903 in service during 1939 and is noteworthy for the weathering effect around the door opening.
Photograph A. E. West

Plate 71 illustrates M264131 in light grey BR livery as running in 1964. This picture has been included as it clearly displays the end bracing, common on these vans.
Photograph Author's Collection

D1828 GOODS VAN

Drawing No. 13/1646   **Figure 30**

D1828
Code: V
Tare: 7 tons 13 cwt
Carrying capacity: 12 tons
Hand brake
Sliding door each side
Steel body with wood lining
Lots 484, 486

D1830 GOODS VAN

Drawing No. 13/1617   **Figure 31**

1,000 steel vans were built by the trade during the period 1929/30 and there is some doubt about their allocation to diagram numbers. The lot book reads:-

Lot 484 — 400 Metropolitan C & W Co. Ltd.
Lot 485 — 300 Gloucester
Lot 486 — 150 Charles Roberts
Lot 487 — 150 Pickering

Of these, the 300 Gloucester vehicles were alleged to have been built to drawing No. 13/1617 and allocated to D1829, page 9C. However, the author has a number of photographs which clearly show that several Gloucester built vans had corrugated ends, so some doubt must exist about D1829 and whether any were ever built to that diagram and so these two diagrams D1828 and D1829 will be considered together.

Diagram Book Page 9B

Figure 30

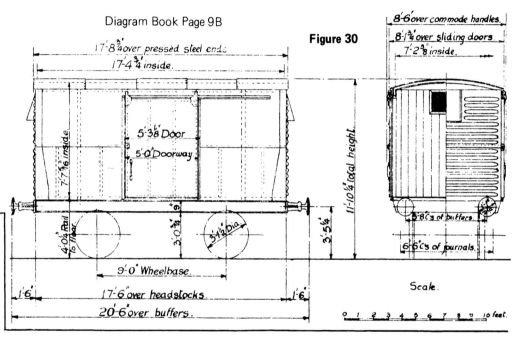

Diagram Book Page 9C

Figure 31

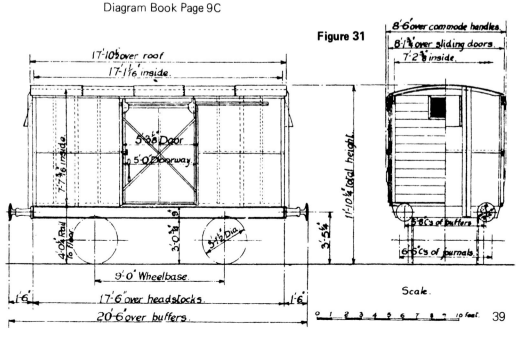

Plate 72

Plate 72 illustrates Gloucester built van No. 186000 in original condition. Other known numbers were: 177779, 183151, 186308, 186851, 186852.

Photograph Gloucester C & W Co. Ltd.

Plate 73

Plate 73 illustrates Gloucester built van No. DM184358 as running c1965 when allocated to a district engineer.

Photograph Author's Collection

Plate 74

Plate 74 This is another example of a Gloucester built van, photographed at Horwich in 1964. At that time, M184882 was in store probably awaiting withdrawal. This picture gives a very good idea of the end construction and it is worth noting that this vehicle still retains its original open spoke wheels.

Photograph Author's Collection

Three other plates have been included but, it has not been possible to be certain which maker produced these vehicles.

Plate 75 illustrates No. 178788 and this van, probably by Pickering, depicts a very different style of door construction when compared with the Gloucester built vans. Indeed, the Gloucester vans have the door construction of D1829 and the ends of D1828, whereas No. 178788 is purely D1828. Other known numbers for this type of vehicle were 147116 and 177675.

Photograph Author's Collection

Plate 76

Plate 75

Plate 76 illustrates No. 197431 with yet a third variety of door construction, built by Charles Roberts. The placing of the legend 'Ventilated Van' should be compared with **Plate 72.**

Photograph Author's Collection

Plate 77

Plate 77 This illustration of No. 190629 is an example of a van built by Charles Roberts and another example probably constructed by this builder is illustrated in **Plate 76.**

Photograph Charles Roberts
Courtesy National Railway Museum

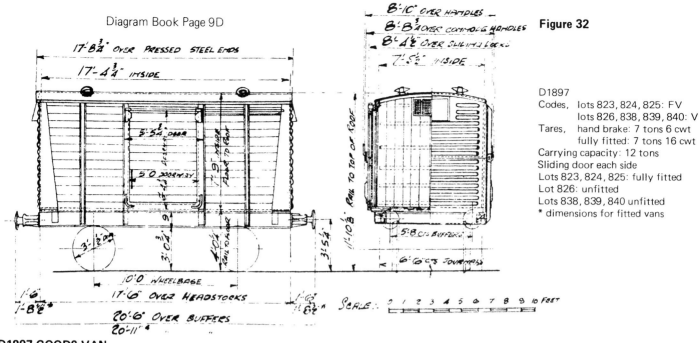

Diagram Book Page 9D

Figure 32

D1897
Codes,   lots 823, 824, 825: FV
         lots 826, 838, 839, 840: V
Tares,   hand brake: 7 tons 6 cwt
         fully fitted: 7 tons 16 cwt
Carrying capacity: 12 tons
Sliding door each side
Lots 823, 824, 825: fully fitted
Lot 826: unfitted
Lots 838, 839, 840 unfitted
* dimensions for fitted vans

D1897 GOODS VAN

Drawing No.	12/277	Lot 823/4/38/39/40	Figure 32
	12/299C	Lot 825/6	
	12/299	Lot 927/8/9	

Running numbers: 506000–508299 fitted; 505800–505999, 503000–505799, 508300–510499, hand brake only.

This large batch of vans, built 1935/6 totalled 7,500 vehicles and the variations noted by the author are recorded on the plates.

Plate 78

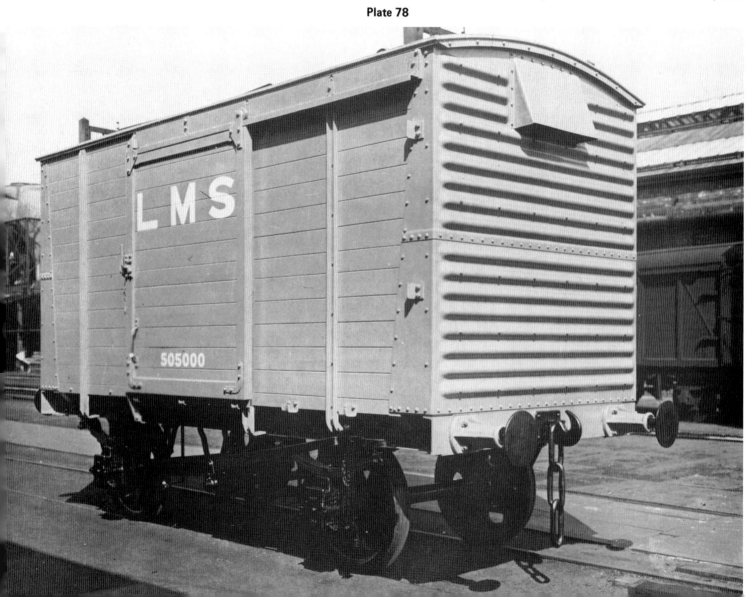

Plate 79 This illustrates van No. 505969 as running in 1938 in grey livery and, although weathered, it clearly depicts the original style of painting.

Photograph A. E. West

Plate 79

Plate 80

Plate 80 This illustrates van No. 510289 in bauxite livery and this photograph shows the livery style of late 1936 which was probably carried by some vehicles until nationalization.

Photograph British Rail

Plate 81 This plate illustrates No. M508587 as running in 1965 and was an example of lot 927 which was originally built as a 'hand brake only' vehicle. However, many unfitted vans were equipped with automatic vacuum brakes by British Railways and here the modifications include a tie bar between the axleboxes and extra diagonal strapping on the sides. This additional strapping was also recorded on Nos. M508560 and M508894 which were both built at 'hand brake only' and were both in the same condition as M508587 by the mid 1960s.

Photograph Author's Collection

◀ **Plate 78** No. 505000 was built to lot 840 and this ex-works picture clearly illustrates a vehicle in pristine condition. It is interesting to note that the roof appears to be in the same colour shade as the van body which, of course, is light grey.

Photograph British Rail

Plate 81

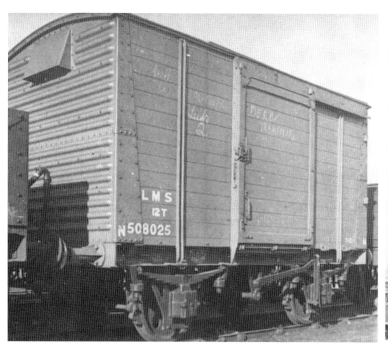

Plate 83

Plates 82 and **83** both depict examples of the final lot No. 929 which consisted of 300 fitted vehicles. What is interesting is that **Plate 82** illustrates No. 508025 in bauxite and was recorded at Buxton on 1st November, 1936, in this condition whereas **Plate 83**, which illustrates No. 508194 with a '20.11.36' paint date visible on the solebar, is in bauxite but with an earlier livery style and it is difficult to provide a logical explanation if the 1st November, 1936, date for No. 508025 is correct.

Photographs, **Plate 82** *Harry Townley*
Plate 83 *British Rail*

Plate 85 This picture of No. 506818 has ▶ been included to illustrate the ex-works paint style on a grey liveried vacuum braked van. Note the white 'X' on the door and 'N' at each end of the van.

Photograph British Rail

Plate 84 This illustrates No. 506150 of lot No. 823 as running in April, 1937. The body colour was dark blue with cream lettering and blue shading.

Photograph British Rail

Plate 84

Plate 85

D1891 GOODS VAN

Diagram Book Page 9E

Drawing No. 12/249 **Figure 33**
12/283 Lot 869 only

Built to lot numbers 766–771/869.

A total of 2,996 vans was allocated to this diagram and all were built during 1934/5, which meant that, unlike D1897 page 9D, these were all turned out in grey livery and many were probably not repainted in bauxite until after the outbreak of World War II.

Running numbers 500000–500999, fitted; 501000–501495, 501500–502999, hand brake only.

As with diagram 1897, this earlier batch of vans incorporates a number of detail differences which are dealt with in the description of the plates.

D1891
Codes, lots 766, 767: FV
lots 768, 769, 770, 771: V
Tares, hand brake: 6 tons 16 cwt
fully fitted: 7 tons 12 cwt
Carrying capacity: 12 tons
'Morton' brake
Sliding door each side
Lots, 766, 767: fully fitted
768, 769, 770, 771: hand brake
* dimensions for fully fitted vans

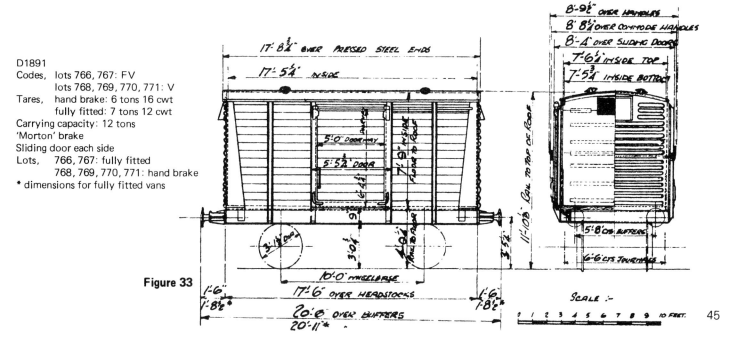

Figure 33

Plate 86

Plate 88

Plate 86 This illustrates No. 501086 with a February 1934 paint date and can therefore be taken as a good example of livery style employed at that time. Note also the spoked wheels.
Photograph British Rail

Plate 87 This example of a fitted van, No. 500714, was built in October 1934 and, being a fitted van, carries the 'N' (non common user) markings and the 'X' on the door; note also the extra strapping clearly visible on the door of this vehicle.
Photograph British Rail

Plate 88 This c1936 picture of van No. 502946 shows a higher positioned 'LMS' on the door, when compared with No. 500714, but is identical to No. 501086, but whereas the earlier vehicle was Derby built this later example was produced at Wolverton and runs on disc, not spoked, wheels.
Photograph G. Y. Hemingway

Plate 87

Plate 89

Plate 89 This illustrates No. 501723 re-liveried in bauxite and is interesting inasmuch as the lettering is closer to the door than one would expect. Regrettably, the date of the photograph is unknown.

Photograph Author's Collection

Plate 91 depicts M501438 in 1964. Note the absence of roof ventilators. This was originally provided with hand brakes only but is now fitted with automatic vacuum brakes and carries a replacement door with vertical, not horizontal, planks.

Photograph Author's Collection

Plate 90 This illustrates the solitary example of lot 869 which also enjoyed a separate drawing and the only difference would appear to be the absence of extra strapping on the door. The paint date on the solebar reads '31.12.34'.

Finally, two BR condition pictures have been included to illustrate the changes which could occur during a vehicle's lifetime.

Plate 92 illustrates M501169, again fitted, but with a tie rod between the axleboxes, no roof ventilators, and no extra strapping on the door which does, however, have vertical planks.

Photograph Author's Collection

17'-8¾" OVER PRESSED STEEL ENDS
17'-5¼" INSIDE
7'-9" FLOOR TO ROOF
5'-5⅞" DOOR
5'-0" DOORWAY
10'-0" WHEELBASE
17'-6" OVER HEADSTOCKS
20'-11" OVER BUFFERS
20' 6"
1'-8½"
1'-6"
4'-6½" ACROSS CORNERS
3'-5¼"

8'-8¼" OVERALL
8'-6⅞" OVER CORNER HANDLES
7'-6¼" INSIDE
11'-8¾" RAIL TO TOP OF ROOF
5'-8" C's OF BUFFERS
6'-4" C's JOURNALS

Figure 34

D1889
Codes, fully fitted: FV
       unfitted: V
Tare: 7 tons 14 cwt
Carrying capacity: 12 tons
'Morton' brake
Sliding door each side
Steel body with plywood panels
Lots 726 ※, 792
※ dimensions for fully fitted vans

Plate 94 The single example of lot 726 is illustrated in this picture, which shows No. 224530 when first constructed.

Photograph British Rail

D1889 GOODS VAN

Diagram Book Page 9F

Drawing No. 12/245

Figure 34

Unlike the earlier steel bodied vans D1828/9, these were built in LMS works and not by the trade and ran on a 10' 0" wheelbase. However, only 5 were built, to two separate lots of 1 and 4, so they must be considered something of an experiment.

The running numbers for lot 792 were 501496–99 and the running number of lot 726 was 224530. It should be noted that this vehicle was fitted with automatic vacuum brakes.

Plate 93 This illustrates van No. 501498 when first built and shows the different style of these later steel vans.

Photograph British Rail

D1978 GOODS VAN   Diagram Book Page 9G   **Plate 94**

Drawing No. 12/332A ⎫
            13/2074D ⎬ Lot 1033   **Figure 35**
            12/332C (Body)
            13/2075 (Underframe) ⎬ Lot 1115–1117
Built to lot numbers 1033/1115–1117.

1,000 fitted vans numbered 510500–511499 and 1,000 hand brake only vans numbered 511500–512499 were built at Wolverton 1937/9 and were all painted in the bauxite livery, never carrying the earlier light grey.

D1978
Codes, fitted: FV
        unfitted: V
Tare:
Carrying capacity: 12 tons
Sliding door each side

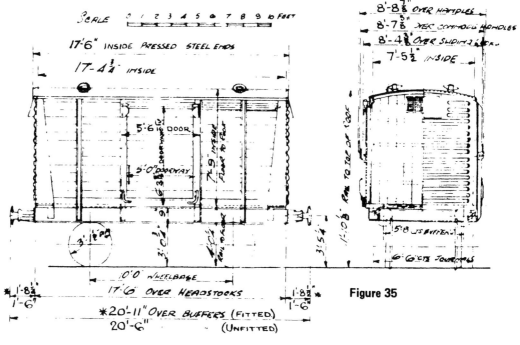

Figure 35

49

Plate 95

At least two of these vans were branded for special traffic and **Plate 95** illustrates No. 511240 as an egg van and **Plate 96** illustrates No. 511246 as a fruit van - both vehicles carrying '11.5.1938' as their painting date. The panels were probably cream or yellow and the lettering black or dark blue.

Photographs British Rail

A non-fitted van for ordinary traffic (No. 511840) is illustrated in **Plate 97** and can be considered typical insofar as the bulk of the construction was concerned. No doubt the majority entered British Railways ownership in this condition.

Photograph British Rail

Plate 96

Plate 97

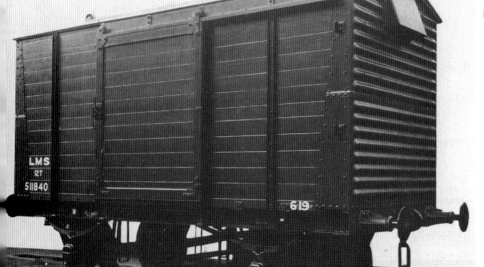

Plate 98 illustrates D2039 van No. 522305 ▶ carrying the smaller size wartime lettering. Note the full length rain strip and roof ventilators.

Photograph British Rail

Drawing No. U/F 13/2075C   **Figure 36**
Body 12/472

Built to lot numbers 1112/1272–1275/Part 1282/1283/
1289/1290/1298/1302/1303/1317/1329/1330/1333/ Part 1338/
Part 1339/Part 1341/1350/1362.

The first of these vehicles was produced in 1940 and construction continued until 1945. Apart from the first batch, numbered
514125–514324, which were fitted, all the remainder were built
with hand brake only and carried running numbers: 512500–
513999 (514325–514720 built by the SR), 515215–515324,
514000–514124, 515325–520133, 520140–521139, 520134–
520139, 522290–522789 in that order of construction.
However, the batch 519140–520133 and 520680–521139
contained some vans built to diagram 2088 (page 9N) and,
unfortunately, the author is unable to confirm just how many
and which numbers went to each diagram. Reference to photographs will reveal the use of two-part and three-part steel ends.
Finally, it should be noted that when fitted by BR with automatic vacuum brakes, the brake pipes were 'coach fashion' and
did not have the LMS 'wagon type' upright pipe.

D2039
Codes, fitted: FV
    unfitted: V
Tare: 7 tons 4 cwt
Carrying capacity: 12 tons
Sliding door each side

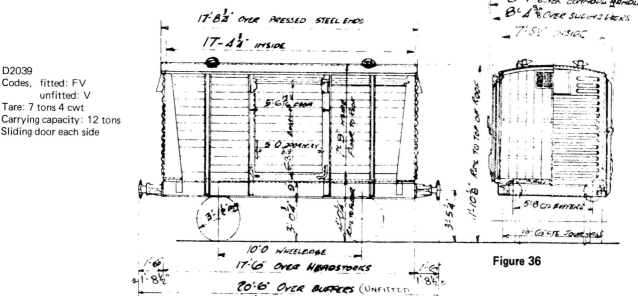

Figure 36

Plate 98

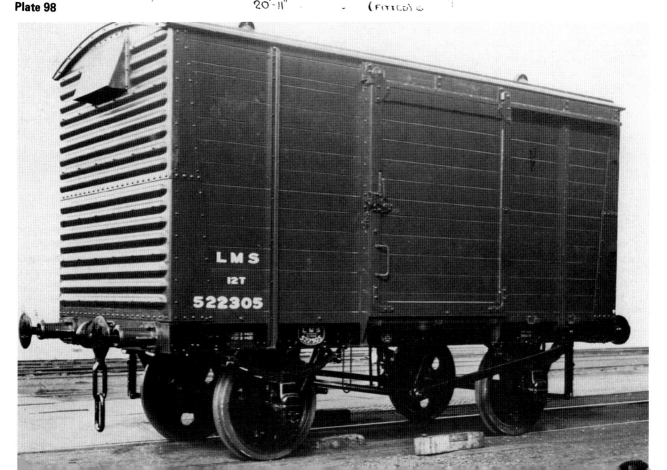

Plate 99 This picture illustrating No. 515140 shows a vehicle built to D2039 but carrying a running number allocated to D2070, page 9J. The location for the photograph is not familiar to the author and may be on the Southern Railway.

Photograph British Rail

Plate 99

Plate 100 This illustrates van No. M522304 in BR condition but, unlike M514053, **Plate 101,** it has retained its roof ventilators, has not acquired extra diagonal body strapping, but, as can be clearly seen, is now fitted with automatic vacuum brakes.

Photograph British Rail

Plate 100

Plate 101

Plate 101 This shows a replacement roof on van No. M514053 as running in 1964. By now, this vehicle has been fitted with automatic vacuum brakes, lost its roof ventilators and acquired extra diagonal strapping on the bodyside. Note the three-part steel pressed ends.

Photograph Author's Collection

The official photograph of the D2070 design appears in **Plate 102** and carries a June 1942 paint date.

Photograph British Rail

D2070 GOODS VAN   Figure 37

Drawing Number not recorded

Built to lot number Part 1282.

494 vans were built by the Southern Railway for the LMS in 1942 and allocated to this diagram with running numbers 514721–515214.

The drawing number given in the lot book refers to the balance of lot of 890 vehicles which were part of D2039, page 9H.

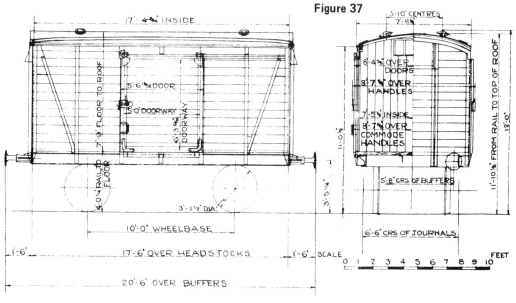

Figure 37

D2070
Code: V
Tare: 7 tons 3 cwt

Carrying capacity: 12 tons
'Morton' brake
Sliding door each side

Plate 102

Plate 103

Plate 103 This illustrates van No. M514966 as running in 1964 after it had been fitted with an automatic vacuum brake by BR and provided with tie rods between the axleboxes.

Photograph Author's Collection

D2079 GOODS VAN

Diagram Book Page 9 K

Drawing number not recorded

Figure 38

250 vans were built by the LNER in 1942 to lot 1335 and carried running numbers 521290—512539 and were the only vehicles allocated to D2079. These vans were, in effect, LNER vehicles in LMS livery, even the axleboxes were marked LNER and were that Company's pattern.

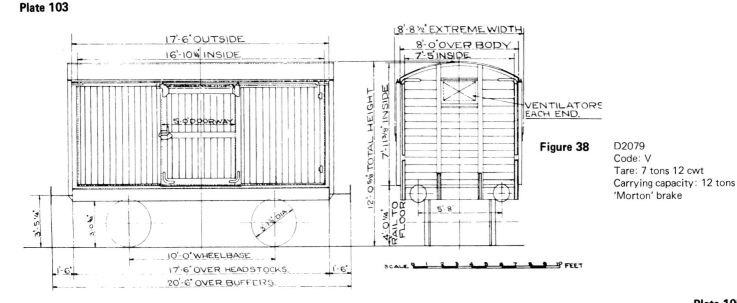

Figure 38

D2079
Code: V
Tare: 7 tons 12 cwt
Carrying capacity: 12 tons
'Morton' brake

Plate 105

Plate 104 illustrates No. 521290 with an October 1942 paint date.

Photograph British Rail

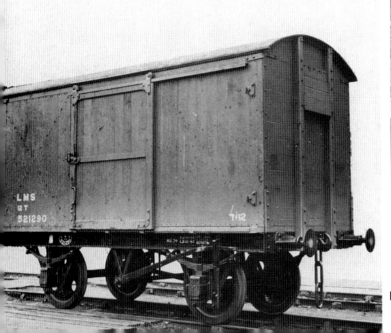

Plate 104

Plate 105 illustrates M521377 in BR livery, having been equipped with axlebox tie rods and fitted with automatic vacuum brakes.

Photograph D. Larkin

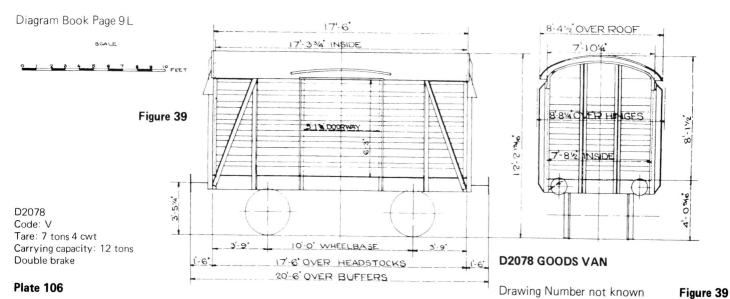

SCALE

0 1 2 3 4 5 6 7 8 9 10 FEET

Figure 39

17'-6"
17'-3¾" INSIDE
5'-1½" DOORWAY
6'-3"
3'-5¼"
3'-9"   10'-0" WHEELBASE   3'-9"
1'-6"   17'-6" OVER HEADSTOCKS   1'-6"
20'-6" OVER BUFFERS

8'-4½" OVER ROOF
7'-10¼"
8'-8¼" OVER HINGES
7'-8½" INSIDE
12'-2 13/16"
8'-1½"
4'-0 5/16"

D2078
Code: V
Tare: 7 tons 4 cwt
Carrying capacity: 12 tons
Double brake

Plate 106

D2078 GOODS VAN

Drawing Number not known   **Figure 39**

400 vans were built in two lots 1334/1373 by the Southern Railway in 1942/44 carrying the running numbers 521140–521289 and 523290–523539. They appear to be a standard Southern design and no details of any drawing numbers were contained in the lot book.

Plate 106 illustrates van No. 521202 of the 1942 batch in original condition.
Photograph British Rail

Plate 107 shows M523370 of the 1944 batch as altered by British Railways and running in 1964. Note the fitting of Morton brakes when equipped with automatic vacuum brakegear and a tie rod between the axleboxes.

Photograph Author's Collection

D2074 GOODS VAN (NCC)

Diagram Book Page 9M

Drawing No. 13/3447

Figure 40

Built to lot number 1326.

This is a very interesting diagram. Firstly, these vehicles only run in Northern Ireland on the 5' 0" gauge system; secondly, they were built by the LNER using a new drawing, thirdly, they are to all intents and purposes, apart from the extra width, identical to 200 vans built by the Midland Railway in 1919 with 'non-standard Midland' side bracing and referred to in *An Illustrated History of Midland Wagons, Volume One,* page 135.

Regrettably, no pictures are known to exist but their NCC running numbers were 2401–2500.

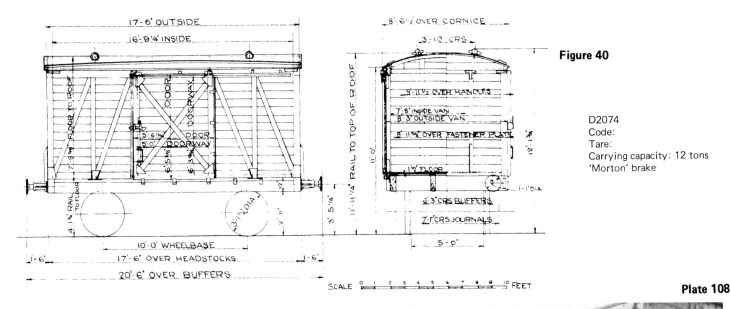

Figure 40

D2074
Code:
Tare:
Carrying capacity: 12 tons
'Morton' brake

Plate 108

D2088 GOODS VAN

Diagram Book Page 9N

Drawing No. 12/472EB

Figure 41

Built to lot number Part 1338/1339/1341 & lot 1354.

This wartime construction of part lots 1338/9/41 and referred to with D2039 page 9H, also included 850 vans built to lot 1354 at Wolverton in 1943 - running numbers 521540–521849 were recorded as amongst those allocated to this batch. In many respects, they were similar to D2070, page 9J, with the principal visible difference being the method of bracing the sides and ends of the vehicle.

No official photographs are known to exist and **Plate 108** which illustrates M521120 (whose number is outside the block given above but inside the numbering block for D2039, page 9H) is the only picture known to the author.

Plate 108 illustrates M521120 as running c1963.

Photograph P. G. Gomm

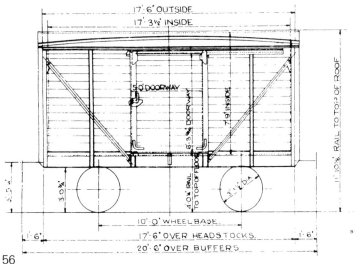

Figure 41

D2088
Code: V
Tare: 7 tons 7 cwt
Carrying capacity: 12 tons
'Morton' brake

D2097 GOODS VAN

Drawing No. U/frame 13/3579
Body 13/3586

Figure 42

A total of 440 vehicles was built in 1944 to lot 1361 with allocated running numbers 521850—522289. Unlike the similar vans allocated to D2108, the vehicles built to D2097 were without roof ventilators. No pictures are known to the author showing these vans in LMS livery.

Plate 109 illustrates van No. M521893 as running in 1965 and equipped with automatic vacuum brakes.

Photograph Author's Collection

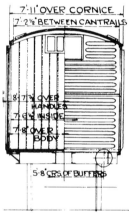

Figure 42

D2097
Code: V
Tare: 7 tons 2 cwt
Carrying capacity: 12 tons
'Morton' brake

Plate 110 illustrates M522212 as running in 1964 and equipped with automatic vacuum brakes and tie rods between the axleboxes. However the most noticeable difference since it was first built is in the door construction, and this should be compared with **Plate 109**.

Photograph Author's Collection

Plate 110

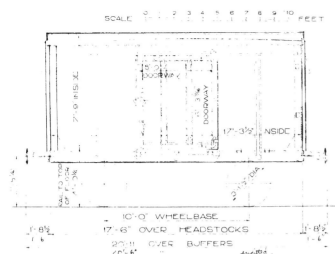

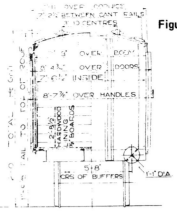

SCALE 0 1 2 3 4 5 6 7 8 9 10 FEET

Figure 43   Diagram Book Page 9Q

D2103
Code: FV
Tare: 7 tons 12 cwt
Carrying capacity: 12 tons
Fully fitted
'Morton' brake

Plate 111

D2103 GOODS VAN

Drawing No. U/frame 13/3652   **Figure 43**
Body 13/3497

Built to lot numbers 1372/1383

During 1945/6 a total of 2,094 vehicles was built at Derby and Wolverton with running numbers 522790–523289 and 523540–525133. Both fitted and hand brake only vans were built, and without doubt during British Railways ownership many unfitted vehicles were equipped with automatic vacuum brakes.

Plate 111 This illustrates No. 523053 as built in January 1946 and is a hand brake only vehicle.

Photograph British Rail

Plate 112 This illustrates van No. 524034 as built in March 1945 and, like No. 523053, is carrying the small wartime size insignia.

Photograph British Rail

Plate 112

Plate 113 M524876 illustrated in this plate carries the 'M' prefix and is labelled 'FISH'. It is not known how many were allocated for this traffic.

Photograph Loco & General

D2112 GOODS VAN (FRUIT AND VEGETABLE)

Drawing No. U/frame 13/3613
Body 13/3497

Built to lot number 1430.

Diagram Book Page 9R

D2112
Code: V
Tare: 8 tons 2 cwt
Carrying capacity: 12 tons
Fully fitted
'Morton' brake

Figure 44

Only 6 vans were specially equipped for fruit and vegetable traffic and allocated to this diagram, carrying running numbers 525134—9. Note the extra roof ventilators. Although not visible on the photographs, the vacuum brake pipes were identical to those illustrated in **Plate 100,** No. 524034.

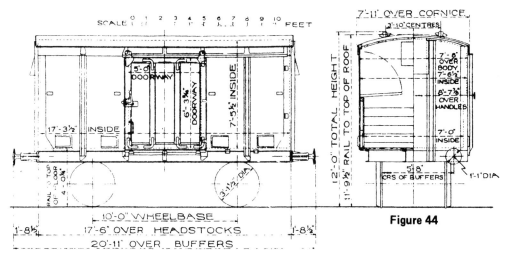

Figure 44

Plate 114

Two views, **Plate Nos. 114** and **115**, have been selected to illustrate these vehicles — both pictures being taken shortly after their construction.

Photographs British Rail

Plate 115

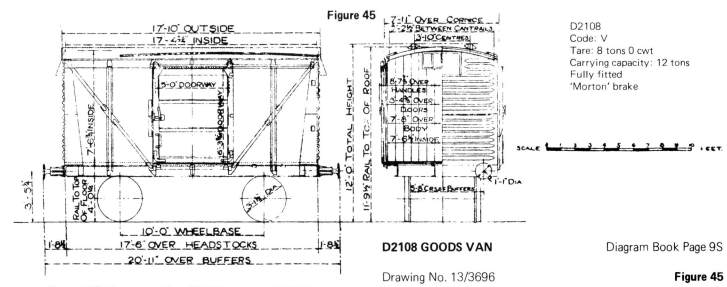

Figure 45

17-10" OUTSIDE
17-4¾" INSIDE

5-0" DOORWAY

7-6¾" INSIDE

6-3¾" DOORWAY

RAIL TO TOP OF FLOOR 4-0¼"

3-7⅞" DIA.

3-5¼"

10-0" WHEELBASE
17-6" OVER HEADSTOCKS
20-11" OVER BUFFERS
1-8½"   1-8½"

7-11" OVER CORNICE
2½" BETWEEN CANTRAILS
3-10" CENTRES

12-0" TOTAL HEIGHT

11-9½" RAIL TO TOP OF ROOF

8-7½" OVER HANDLES
9-4⅞" OVER DOORS
7-8" OVER BODY
7-6" INSIDE

5-8" C/RS OF BUFFERS

1-1" DIA.

D2108
Code: V
Tare: 8 tons 0 cwt
Carrying capacity: 12 tons
Fully fitted
'Morton' brake

SCALE |1|2|3|4|5|6|7|8|9|10| FEET.

D2108 GOODS VAN

Drawing No. 13/3696

Diagram Book Page 9S

Figure 45

Plate 116 illustrates No. 525333 branded 'FISH' and carrying a March 1946 paint date and some doubt must exist as to whether it was built in that year or if it was built and then later allocated to fish traffic. In addition No. 524960 was also branded 'FISH'.

Photograph British Rail

Built to lot number 1413.

Totalling 1350 vehicles, these vans were all equipped with automatic vacuum brakes and carried running numbers 525140—526489, being ordered in 1944 but probably were not all completed until 1946.

Plate 116

Plate 117 This illustrates van No. 526185 in its original condition and carries a June 1946 paint date.

Photograph British Rail

Plate 118

Plate 118 This illustrates M525261 and, when photographed, carried a 'Built Wolverton 1946' plate which tends to suggest that this lot, ordered in 1944, was not completed until 1946. If this recording of 1946 is correct, it would suggest that No. 525333, **Plate 116,** was built as a fish van.

Photograph Author's Collection

Plate 117

Diagram Book Page 9T

D2149 GOODS VAN

Drawing No.   **Figure 46**
Gloucester 29045A

Both the lot book and the diagram record these vans as lot 1596 and the diagram states 'purchased from MoS' (Ministry of Supply). The lot book gives the quantity as 4 vehicles but no running numbers are known as these vans appear to have been acquired by British Railways in 1949.

No pictures of these vehicles are known to exist.

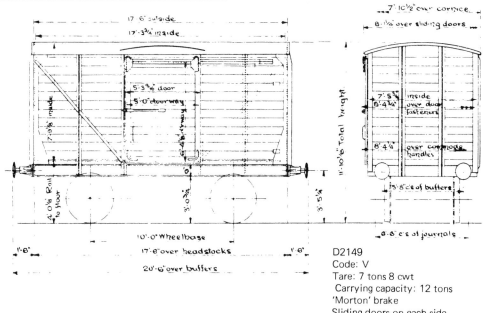

D2149
Code: V
Tare: 7 tons 8 cwt
Carrying capacity: 12 tons
'Morton' brake
Sliding doors on each side
Lot 1596

Figure 46

D1665 GUNPOWDER VAN   Diagram Book Page 10

Drawing No. RCH No. P0178 lot 27/109/415   **Figure 47**
14/2050 lot 709
14/2050C lot 923
14/2050E lot 1027

Built to lot numbers 27/109/415/709/923/1027/1200.

As recorded above, the earliest vehicles were built to an RCH drawing but later in 1933, an LMS drawing was issued. These vans were built between 1923 and 1939 and the earliest construction, which totalled 95 vehicles, carried random running numbers, of which 287211, 299031 and 299042 are known. The 1936/39 construction, which totalled 65 vans, was numbered 701000–64 and it is believed that the first 20 were painted grey - see **Plate 122**. All other construction from No. 701020 upwards was probably painted bauxite from new.

Plate 119 This picture of No. 299031, taken just prior to the vehicle entering traffic in November 1933, is interesting in so far as it is the only picture known to the author showing the early LMS livery style on a grey vehicle. It is thought that this painting style would have been applied to all the vehicles which carried the random numbers when built.

Photograph British Rail

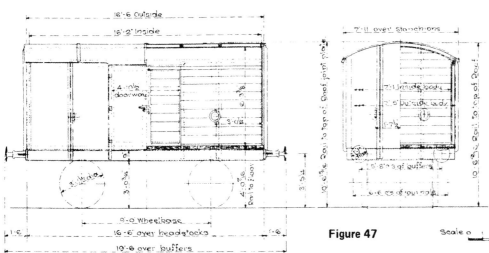

D1665
Code: GPV
Tare: 8 tons 1 cwt
Carrying capacity: 7 tons
Double brake

Figure 47   Scale 0 1 2 3 4 5 6 7 8 9 10 feet.

Plate 120 This illustrates No. M287211 of lot 415 in British Railways livery and it will be noted that this van is now equipped with automatic vacuum brakes and a tie rod between the axleboxes. It is also interesting to note that it has single vee hangers and heavy buffers when compared with **Plates 119, 121** and **122.**

Photograph D. Larkin

Plate 121 No. M299042 of lot 709 is seen in British Railways livery and, like the vehicle pictured in **Plate 119,** is equipped with through vacuum brake pipes.

Photograph D. Larkin

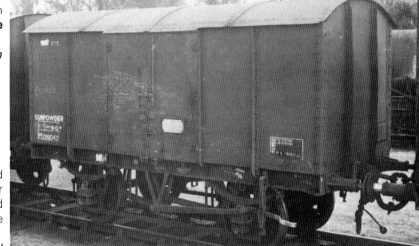

Plate 122 This depicts No. 701018 of lot 923 and carried a September 1936 painted date. The body colour is grey but the size and position of 'LMS' '7 T' and running number is that normally associated with the bauxite livery.

Photograph British Rail

Plate 123

D2093 GUNPOWDER VAN   Diagram Book Page 10A

Drawing No. 14/3882 lots 1337/49   **Figure 48**
14/4313A lot 1474

Built to lot numbers 1337/1349/1474.

Unlike the vans built to D1665, these vehicles were rated at 11 tons on the diagram, not the 7 tons of D1665, although as noted, the D1665 vehicles were later uprated to this higher carrying capacity.

A total of 55 vehicles were constructed at Wolverton between 1943–1948. In 1943 Nos. 701065–84 were built and the following years saw the production of Nos. 260928–47 for the LNER with a final batch numbered 701085–701099 being produced in 1948 by British Railways.

Plate 124 This illustrates No. 260930 in LNER livery when constructed in 1944. No other pictures of these vans in LMS or British Railways livery are known to the author. The vehicles built for the LNER were painted lead colour for body and body ironwork, black for wheels, axles, brakegear, steel underframes and all other underframe ironwork. All writing was to be white. The gunpowder van identification mark was a 6″ diameter circle in white with a 5″ diameter inner circle in black with a white letter in a 3″ diameter circle.

Photograph British Rail

Plate 124

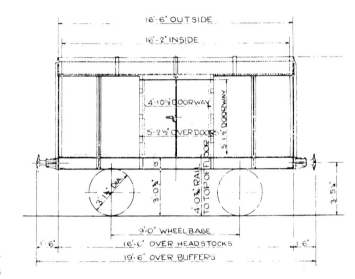

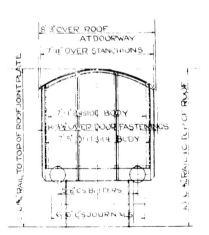

Figure 48

D2093
Code: GPV
Tare: 8 tons
Carrying capacity: 11 tons
Double brake

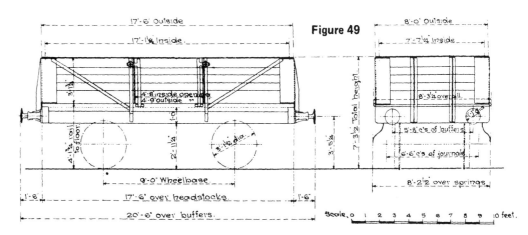

Figure 49

D1666
Code: HG
Tare: 6 tons 19 cwt
Carrying capacity: 12 tons
Cubic capacity: 408 cu. ft.
Double brake
Door on each side

D1666 HIGH-SIDED GOODS WAGON

Drawing No. 5612   **Figure 49**

Built to lot numbers: 1005 (Midland Railway lot); LMS lots 6/17–19/67/68/84/89/92/110/116/117/140/151/205/221/226/240/296/301/323/339/350/362/376/393/413/426/427/438/439/470/471/482/483/515/535/547/548/590.

The first vehicles built to this Midland Railway drawing were to a Midland Railway lot, number 1005, and these 1,000 vehicles marked the beginning of a surge of construction which covered the period 1923–1930 and saw the completion of 54,450 'open goods' to this diagram. No block numbers were employed but, fortunately, examination of many photographs, has enabled a considerable quantity to be compiled for the use of modellers.

Known running numbers included: 24361, 54680, 91919, 92978, 96653, 113012, 114872, 122580, 130487, 133488, 134571, 139905, 140086, 153532, 156239, 157511, 158124/5, 159093, 169147, 170901, 179352, 197803, 216051, 217624, 234421, 237015, 238611, 247185, 247422, 282102, 304008, 315033, 327674, 331426, 344839, 348708, 360790.

A number of plates have been selected to illustrate the various livery styles carried by these vehicles from the earliest LMS period until their withdrawal by British Railways.

Plate 125 This illustrates No. 24361 which carries a December 1923 paint date. Note the absence of '12T', the location of the tare weight on the solebar and the disc wheels. Without doubt, this vehicle is from lot 1005.

Photograph British Rail

Plate 125

Plate 127

Plate 126 This illustration of No. 247185 reveals a number of differences when compared with **Plate 125:** the tare weight is now on the bodyside, solid spoke, not disc, wheels are provided, and there is a different angle on the T stanchions on the ends of the vehicle.

Photograph British Rail

Plate 127 depicts the 'grey' livery some ten years after construction. Photographed in 1938 No. 304008 now has the tare weight on the right hand end and the '12T' over the vehicle number and this painting has taken place since the vehicle was built, whereas the general condition of the paintwork and almost total loss of the 'LMS' suggests that No. 304008 has yet to have its first repaint. Note also the disc wheels.

Photograph A. E. West

Plate 128

Plate 129 This interesting picture of No. 96653 has been included to show some of the interior detail of D1666 vehicles. On the original print the top cornerplate and four vertical pieces of ironwork can clearly be seen together with the ironwork inside the door. In addition two pieces of ironwork were to be found behind the upright pieces by the side of the door.

Photograph British Rail

Plate 129

Plate 130

Plate 130 No. 217624 photographed in September 1938 has been repainted in bauxite livery and carries the new style lettering.

Photograph A. E. West

◄ **Plate 128** No. 158124 has been included to show new 1929 construction but in particular the photographic livery which highlights the brake gear.

Photograph British Rail

Plate 131

Plate 131 This interesting wartime picture is dated December 1939 and the first wagon, No. 139905, painted in bauxite, has been uprated to carry 13T, in accordance with the new practice introduced just after the outbreak of the Second World War. The second vehicle is an ex-LYR open goods in use for coal traffic.

Photograph British Rail

Plate 132 This illustration of M234421 illustrates BR partly painted, partly unpainted livery. The wagon has been marked 'on loan to CCE' and also 'COND' (condemned).

Photograph D. P. Rowland

Plate 134 This illustrates No. 402854 in original condition. Note the lack of '12T' on the bodyside and use of disc wheels. Compare the door stops with wagon No. 413833 in **Plate 135**.

Photograph British Rail

Plate 133 This final picture, dated 1967, shows No. M113012 en route to Crewe with a train of loco coal. Many of these vehicles were used for loco coal traffic prior to withdrawal. Note the large 'COND' above 'Loco Coal' at the right hand end.

Photograph Author's Collection

D1895 12 TON HIGH-SIDED GOODS WAGON
WOOD UNDERFRAME   Diagram Book Page 11A

Drawing No. 13/2038 lots 807/8   **Figure 50**
            13/2654A lot 1118

Built to lot numbers 807/808/1118.

The official records show that 1,200 wagons numbered 402000-403199 were built to the first two lots and that 800 were built to lot 1118 carrying the numbers 413650—414449. However, lot 1118 is shown in the lot book as D1896 but photographs and the official drawing suggests they were really D1895, although with minor differences to the first two lots constructed. Lots 807/8 were built in 1934, lot 1118 was built in 1938/9.

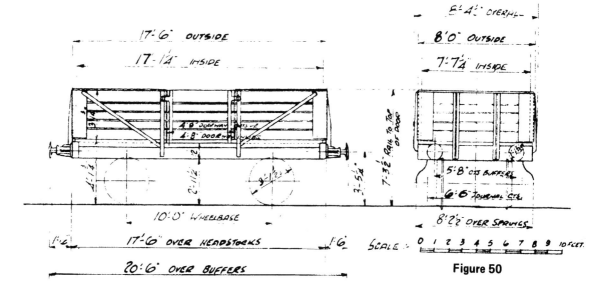

D1895
Code: HG
Tare: 6 tons 19 cwt
Carrying capacity: 12 tons
Cubic capacity: 408 cu. ft.
'Morton' brake: lot 808
Double brake: lot 807
Door on each side
Lots 807, 808

Figure 50

Plate 135

Plate 135 This 1938 picture of No. 413833 of lot 1118 clearly displays the bauxite livery of that period and establishes that this batch was in fact D1895.

Photograph A. E. West

Plate 136 This picture shows DM402240 rated to carry 13 tons and allocated to departmental stock with a 'D' prefix. Photographed in 1964, it displays the typical 'unpainted livery' of that period.

Photograph Author's Collection

Plate 136

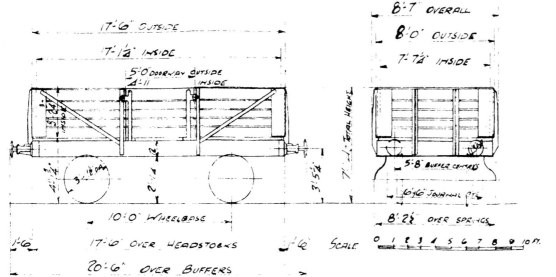

D1896
Code: HGK
Tare: 6 tons 10 cwt
Carrying capacity: 12 tons
Cubic capacity: 408 cu. ft.
'Morton' type hand brake
Door on each side
Lot 809

Figure 51

Plate 137

D1896 12TON OPEN GOODS WAGON

Drawing No. 13/2046   **Figure 51**

For some reason, a batch of 700 wagons numbered 403200–403899 were built at Derby in 1934 to lot 809 and were without curb rails - compare **Plate 134** of D1895 with **Plate 137** of D1896 and note the absence of the wooden rail which runs across the length of the side at the bottom of D1895, in contrast to D1896. No pictures are known to exist of these wagons showing LMS livery but it would have been grey when first constructed, identical in layout to D1895 and repainting in bauxite would have begun c1939. Two pictures have been selected to display BR livery and detail alterations.

Plate 137 This illustrates No. 403290 with a 'DM' prefix, photographed in 1965.
Photograph Author's Collection

Plate 138

Plate 138 This 1965 picture illustrates No. M403606 with a small 'D' prefix, as well as 'EM', on black patches upon an otherwise unpainted body. However, the points to note are spoked wheels and the end steelwork modification. It is not known when this was done or how many vehicles were so treated.
Photograph Author's Collection

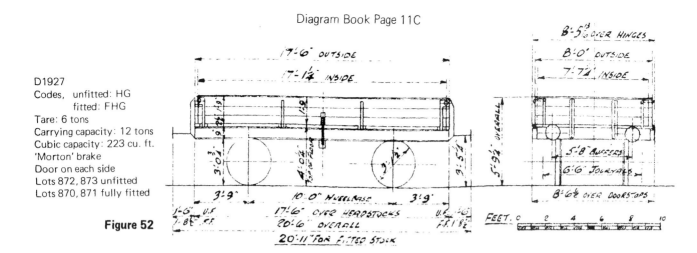

D1927

Codes, unfitted: HG
fitted: FHG
Tare: 6 tons
Carrying capacity: 12 tons
Cubic capacity: 223 cu. ft.
'Morton' brake
Door on each side
Lots 872, 873 unfitted
Lots 870, 871 fully fitted

Figure 52

D1927 12 TON MEDIUM GOODS WAGON
STEEL UNDERFRAME

Drawing No. 13/2051 Fitted lot 870/1   **Figure 52**
13/2055A Handbrake only lot 872/3
13/2323 Fitted lot 920
13/2322A Handbrake only lot 921/2/30
13/2322 Fitted lot 970
13/2322C lot 1013/4/5
13/2323F lot 1135/36/37
13/3618A lot 1382
13/3680 lot 1417
13/3775A lot 1472/1521
13/4024 lot 1522

Built to lot numbers 870–873/920–922/930/970/ 1013–1015/1135–1137/1382/1417/1472/1521/1522.

This large batch of wagons was built to a variety of drawings and a considerable number were built with automatic vacuum brakes and the running numbers are as follows:-

Fitted with automatic brakes
470000–471099, 471700–471949, 473460–473699, 475700–475849, 477900–480149.

Handbrake only
471100–471699, 471950–473459, 473700–475699, 475850–476349, 476900–477899, 480150–480649.

However, there is some evidence to suggest that the lot book as quoted above may be in error and, apart from wagons later fitted by British Railways, **Plate 141** illustrates wagon No. 473449 of lot 930 which is clearly fitted with an automatic vacuum brake whereas the official records suggest that it was built as a hand brake only vehicle and modellers are recommended to select as models vehicles where they have a picture which clearly shows mechanical condition and running number. Of these wagons, those numbered from about 471700 upwards never ran in grey livery with large 'LMS', while those numbered 478400 upwards were built by BR and came out with 'M' prefixes in an 'unpainted livery' adopted by BR for wooden bodied new construction - see **Plate 144**.

The replacement of pre-grouping medium goods wagons did not begin until 1935 and then 10,100 were constructed to this diagram by 1949 and a further 550 to a similar diagram D2101.

Many of these vehicles were still running in departmental stock in the late 1970s and a number of pictures have been selected to illustrate the variations recorded by the author.

Plate 139 This picture of No. 471405 is the only known illustration of an ex-works grey liveried wagon. This example was built by Charles Roberts in 1935.

Photograph Charles Roberts

Plate 139

Plate 140 This c1938 illustration shows No. 471424 in service.

Photograph G. Y. Hemingway

Plate 141 This ex-works picture shows No. 473449 of lot 930 which was numbered 473210—473459 and it can clearly be seen that the wagon was fitted with automatic vacuum brake, whereas the above information, from official sources, records that this lot was 'hand brake only'.

Photograph British Rail

Plate 142 This picture of No. 474990 was taken in 1939 and the wagon, built in 1937, appears to be in grey livery but with the small size insignia normally associated with the bauxite livery. In 1937 a number of wagons were painted grey but with the small size 'LMS' insignia, a fact discussed in greater depth in the livery chapter in *Volume 2*. However, whilst it is likely that the information given above is correct inasmuch as large 'LMS' on the body-side is concerned, the author is unable to say when the correct small 'LMS' and bauxite colour began. Finally, readers will note that No. 473449 is in bauxite while No. 474990 is grey and this is explained by the fact that both vehicles were built in 1936, with No. 473449 being the late part of a Wolverton lot while No. 474990 is the early part of a Charles Roberts lot.

Photograph A. E. West

Plate 143 In this picture No. 471088 has been uprated to 13T carrying capacity and carries the wartime 'unpainted' livery. All new construction was unpainted wood, apart from the patches where the lettering and numbers were placed.

Photograph British Rail

Plate 143

Plate 144

Plate 144 illustrates No. M480021 and this wagon was built in 1949 to lot 1521 and it will be noted that, unlike other wagons illustrated, No. M480021 displays an extra piece of iron-work on the ends.

Photograph British Rail

Plate 145 This interesting picture displays No. M479505 and this vehicle carries a tarpaulin bar, together with a 'Kentish Town' branding. It is not known how many wagons were so altered.

Photograph Author's Collection

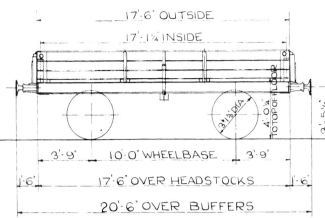

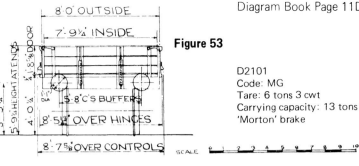

Figure 53

D2101
Code: MG
Tare: 6 tons 3 cwt
Carrying capacity: 13 tons
'Morton' brake

Plate 146 This ex-works picture of No. 476491 is the only illustration known to the author which shows a vehicle from lot 1364.

Photograph British Rail

Plate 147 illustrates No. M480652 in original condition and it is believed they were painted in LMS bauxite. No other pictures are known to exist of these wagons in British Railways livery.

Photograph British Rail

D2101 13 TON MEDIUM GOODS WAGON STEEL UNDERFRAME

Drawing No. 13/3582   **Figure 53** *Above*

One lot only, No. 1364, consisting of 550 wagons built in 1945 and numbered 476350—476899, were allocated to this diagram. The only difference between D2101 and D1927 was that D2101 was built with slightly thinner side and end planks.

D2147 12 TON MEDIUM GOODS WAGON

Drawing No. HN 0/5120A   **Figure 54**

Four wagons allocated running numbers 480650—480653, built to lot No. 1569 were recorded in the lot book as 'altered at Derby' and a further note states that they were 'Purchased from Fowlers'.

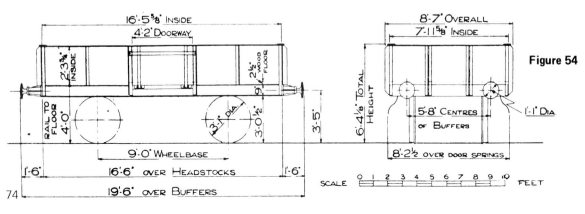

Figure 54

D2147
Code:
Tare: 6 ton 17 cwt
Cubic capacity: 303 cu. ft.
Double brake
Two side doors

D1667
Code: HG
Tare: 6 tons 14 cwt
Carrying capacity: 12 tons
Cubic capacity: 408 cu. ft.
Double brake
Door on each side

Figure 55

D1667 STANDARD HIGH SIDED GOODS WAGON STEEL FRAME

Drawing 5719/5720   **Figure 55**

While the LMS workshops were building thousands of wooden underframe wagons the trade built 5,500 vehicles during 1924–1928 and then Newton Heath built a further 2,500 during 1929/30. No block numbers were used and the following random numbers were recorded: 85457, 85698, 94980, 104838, 109621, 130042, 135109, 141354, 229769, 283664, 290553, 295015, 303471, 322789, 323555, 338968.

The livery styles were similar to that described for other open goods wagons, in particular, D1666 page 11, and four pictures have been selected to illustrate these vehicles.

Plate 148 This picture shows wagon No. 85698 when first built and the location of the tare weight at the extreme left hand end is interesting. No. 130042, built by G. R. Turner, had its number on the same plank as No. 85698 but further to the left with the tare '6-12-3' below, but hard against the diagonal strapping.

Photograph British Rail

Plate 149 This ex-works picture of No. 141354, shows the 'as new' livery of a Metropolitan Wagon & Carriage Co. vehicle. Compare running number and tare weight with **Plate 148**. These locations varied according to builder.

Photograph HMRS Collection

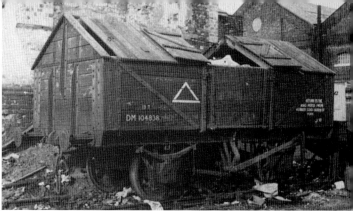

Plate 150 No. M338968 was photographed in 1964 and was originally built in 1927 by Hall, Lewis & Co. of Cardiff. It presents a typical 1950s–60s look of wooden bodied open goods wagon with only partly painted woodwork and patches to display numbers, etc.

Photograph Author's Collection

Plate 151 This illustrates a conversion of No. 104838 to depar mental use and a 'DM' prefix. Apart from the white triangle is branded 'Return to the Road Motor Engnr, Rubber Sdg Queen Street, York'. Photographed in 1970.

Photograph J. P. Also

D1839 12 TON MERCHANDISE WAGON STEEL FRAME

Drawing No. 13/1734 **Figure 56**

One lot only was built to this diagram, No. 676, in 1933, which covered 100 wagons with random numbers, although only No. 3466 has been recorded. These 100 fitted wagons were probably for use with the additional express goods trains, introduced during that period. No further steel end fitted open wagons were built until 1946.

Diagram Book Page 12A

D1839
Code: FHG
Tare: 6 tons 17 cwt
Carrying capacity: 12 tons
Cubic capacity: 415 cu. ft.
Fully fitted
Door on each side
Lot 676

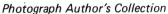

Figure 56

Plate 152 This illustrates wagon No. 3466 i original condition. Regrettably, no othe pictures of this type are known to exist.

Photograph British Ra

Diagram Book Page 12B **Figure 57**

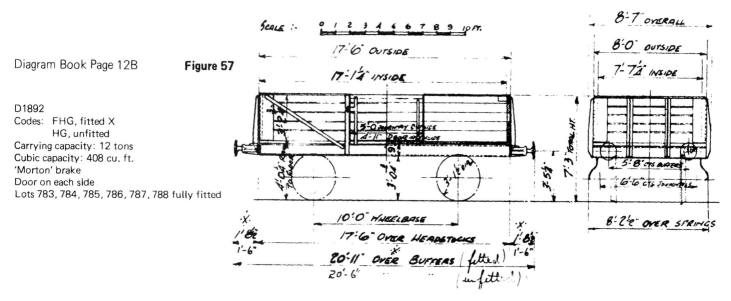

D1892
Codes: FHG, fitted X
HG, unfitted
Carrying capacity: 12 tons
Cubic capacity: 408 cu. ft.
'Morton' brake
Door on each side
Lots 783, 784, 785, 786, 787, 788 fully fitted

D1892 12 TON MERCHANDISE WAGON

Drawing No. 13/1960 lots 783–8   **Figure 57**
     13/2118 lot 810
     13/2284 lot 918/957–64, 1003/4, 1024/6/30/1
     132284G lot 1110/1/19

Built to lot numbers 783–788/810/918/957–964/1003/1004/
1024–1026/1030/1031/1110/1111/1119.
Running numbers were as follows:-
Wagons fitted with automatic vacuum brake: 400000–401999,

411250–411749.
Wagons fitted with hand brake only: 404000–409779,
409800–415299.
All wagons up to No. 406749 were completed in grey with the
large 'LMS' on the bodyside while those numbered from 406750
upwards were finished in bauxite with the small 'LMS'. A
quantity of these vehicles were altered to oxygen cylinder
wagons, D2047 page 66, and airscrew wagons, D2057 page 12C.
In view of the large number of wagons built (12,200 in total
between 1934–1939), several pictures have been selected to
illustrate various conditions of these vehicles.

Plate 153 This picture of No. 400231 is the solitary example of lot 810 and why
just one vehicle was built to drawing 13/2118 is not known.

Photograph British Rail   **Plate 153**

Plate 154 This ex-works picture of No.404104 clearly shows the January 1936 livery in use during this period.

Photograph British Rail

Plate 155 No. 405268 photographed in 1938 illustrates the opposite side of a hand brake only wagon and should be compared with **Plate 154.**

Photograph A. E. West

Plate 156 This view illustrates a Gloucester Carriage & Wagon Company built vehicle No. 406644, and, apart from showing one of the last wagons to be turned out in grey with large letters, the picture has been included to show the end construction of these vehicles.

Photograph Gloucester Carriage & Wagon Co.

Plate 157 This picture illustrates No. 401486 in service, c1938.

Photograph R. Pochin

Plate 155

Plate 156   **Plate 157**

Plate 158 Photographed in 1938, No. 412017 is seen in service loaded with coal, and proves that the British Railways custom of c1950 of using merchandise wagons for coal traffic was a pre-war practice.

Photograph A. E. West

Plate 158

Plate 159 This picture of No. 401204 shows the as-built condition of one of the fitted vehicles constructed by Charles Roberts in 1934. The white tyres were probably for photographic purposes.

Photograph Charles Roberts

Plate 159

Plate 160 Finally, No. M400547, photographed in 1964, provides an example of a fitted wagon in BR days; it will be noted that new steel ends have been fitted to the wagon.

Photograph Author's Collection

Plate 160

D2057 IMPROVISED AIR SCREW WAGON

Converted from D1893
(page 12B, in 1940)

Figure 58

A simple wartime modification saw the provision of fixed wooden cradles to carry crated aircraft propellers. It is probable that these converted wagons reverted to their original purposes after the war. No pictures are known to exist showing these conversions.

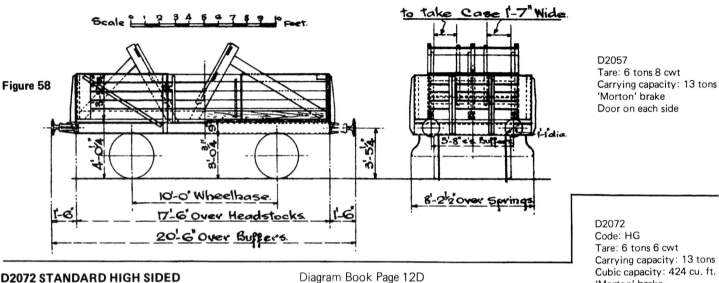

Figure 58

D2057
Tare: 6 tons 8 cwt
Carrying capacity: 13 tons
'Morton' brake
Door on each side

D2072
Code: HG
Tare: 6 tons 6 cwt
Carrying capacity: 13 tons
Cubic capacity: 424 cu. ft.
'Morton' brake
Door on each side

D2072 STANDARD HIGH SIDED GOODS WAGON

Drawing No. 13/3364   **Figure 59**

500 wagons numbered 415300–415799 to lot 1322 were produced at Derby and Wolverton during 1942/3 and were generally similar to D1892, except that thinner planks were used for the sides and ends.

No official photographs were taken and no pictures of these wagons in British Railways livery are known to the author; however, they would have been similar to other contemporary construction. See wagon No. 418900 **Plate 161.**

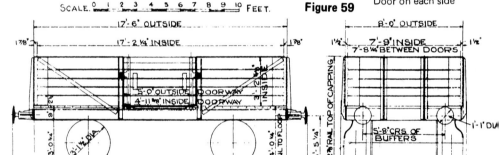

Figure 59

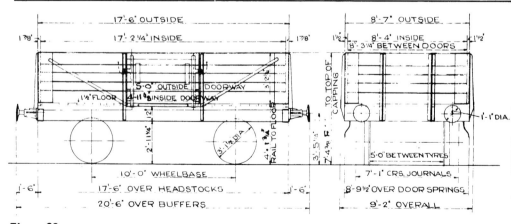

D2073 HIGH SIDED GOODS WAGON (NCC)

Drawing 13/3439   **Figure 60**

These broad gauge wagons for the NCC totalled over 150 and were built by the LNER to lot 1325, probably in 1942, as part of the overall wartime building procedure whereupon vehicles were built by one Company for another.

Regrettably, no photographs are known to the author showing them in any livery.

Figure 60

D2073
Code:
Tare:
Carrying capacity: 12 tons

Cubic capacity: 457 cu. ft.
'Morton' brake
Door on each side

Figure 61

D2094
Code: HG
Tare: 6 tons 7 cwt
Carrying capacity: 13 tons
Cubic capacity: 427 cu. ft.
'Morton' brake
Door on each side

Plate 161

D2094 STANDARD HIGH SIDED GOODS WAGON   Diagram Book Page 12F

Drawing No. 13/3496   **Figure 61**
13/3696A
13/3226 U/frame

Built to lot numbers 1345/1353/1371/1381/1394.

3,775 wagons were built at Derby and Wolverton during 1943/46 and were numbered 415800—419574. They were generally similar to D1892 and were probably all constructed in the unpainted livery shown in **Plate 161.**

Plate 161 This illustrates wagon No. 418900 of lot 1394 built in 1946. Note the unpainted livery which was normal practice during this period for many common user vehicles, as was the 13T rating.

Photograph British Rail

Plate 162 This illustrates a British Railways Hybar conversion, wagon No. M419181, now fitted with a tarpaulin bar, tie rods between the axleboxes and automatic vacuum brakes. Photographed at Camden c1962.

Photograph British Rail

Plate 163 This also illustrates a Hybar conversion to wagon No. M416787, similar to **Plate 162** but without tie bars. A further picture exists showing M419278 in identical condition to M419181.

Photograph Author's Collection

D2110 HIGH SIDED GOODS WAGON

Drawing No. 13/3684   **Figure 62**
           13/3768
           13/3901

Built to lot numbers 1416/1420/1453/1464/1473.

3,550 wagons were built between 1946—48 and carried running numbers 419575—423124 and, within this batch, 422375—422624 were fitted with automatic vacuum brakes when first constructed. These vehicles had pressed steel ends and were the first wagons with steel ends to be built since 1933.

Diagram Book Page 12G

D2110
Codes: HG, unfitted
        FHG, fully fitted *
Tare: 6 tons 12 cwt
Carrying capacity: 13 tons
Cubic capacity: 417 cu. ft.
'Morton' brake
Door on each side

Figure 62

SCALE 0 1 2 3 4 5 6 7 8 9 10 FEET

Plate 164

Plate 165 Wagon No. 422595 of lot 1464, is an example of a vacuum fitted wagon and it is interesting to note that this new vehicle has spoked wheels.

Photograph British Rail

Plate 166 This 1964 view shows wagon No. M420890, originally hand brake only but now running with automatic vacuum brakes. Note the tie rods between the replacement axleboxes.

Photograph Author's Collection

Plate 166

◄ Plate 164 No. 419796 of lot 1416, was built in 1948, and is seen as a hand brake only wagon in final LMS livery. Although British Railways construction would replace the 'LMS' by 'M', no other changes would be evident.

Photograph British Rail

D2150 HIGH SIDED GOODS WAGON

Drawing No. 13/4019C lot 1510
13/4020C lot 1511

Figure 63

These 1,500 wagons were never lettered 'LMS'. 300 to lot 1510 were numbered M423125–M423424 and 1,200 to lot 1511 were numbered M423425–M424624 and **Plates 167** and **168** depict these vehicles when first built.

Diagram Book Page 12H

D2150
Codes: HG, unfitted
FHG, fully fitted*
Tare: 7 tons 5 cwt
Carrying capacity: 13 tons
Cubic capacity: 417 cu. ft.
'Morton' brake
Door on each side

Figure 63

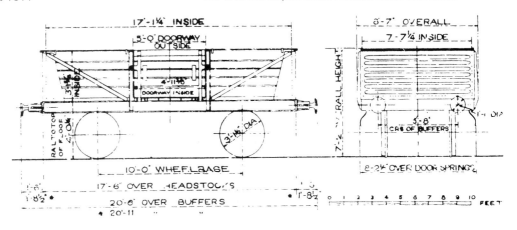

Plate 167 This illustrates wagon No. M423253 of lot 1510 when first constructed in 'unpainted wood' livery.

Photograph British Rail

Plate 167

Plate 168 Wagon No. M424333 is a hand brake only example of lot 1511 in original condition.

Photograph British Rail

Plate 168

Plate 169 This illustrates wagon No. M423401 of lot 1510 in service in 1966.

Photograph D. P. Rowland

Plate 169

Drawing SR E32760 **Figure 64**

A total of 158 wagons came into London Midland Region ownership from the Ministry of Supply and 144 were allocated to lot 1593 with the final 14 to lot 1612. The running numbers were M360120—M360263 and M360358—M360371.

Figure 64

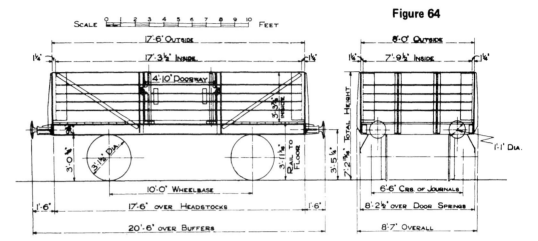

D2151
Code: HG
Tare: 6 tons 3 cwt to 6 tons 12 cwt
Carrying capacity: 13 tons
Cubic capacity: 445 cu. ft.
Brake either side
Door on each side

Plate 170

Plate 170 This illustrates wagon No. M360221 in 1964 after being fitted with automatic vacuum brakes.

Photograph D. P. Rowland

Plate 171

Plate 171 This picture shows wagon No. M360236 in 1965. This wagon has been converted to automatic vacuum brake operation and the reader's attention is drawn to the different axleboxes on M360236 compared with M360221.

Photograph D. P. Rowland

D1668 HOPPER WAGON (LOCO)   Diagram Book Page 13

Drawing EARLESTOWN 894   **Figure 65**

In 1925 50 wagons were built to a LNWR design and carried various numbers. Lot number 149 authorized this construction. No official photographs were taken in 1925 and no photographs are known to the author.

Figure 65

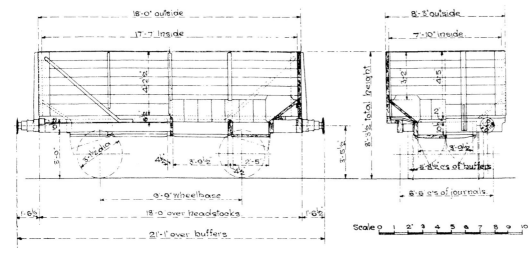

D1668
Code: HPW
Tare: 7 tons 19 cwt
Carrying capacity: 15 tons
Cubic capacity: 585 cu. ft.
Double brake
6 bottom doors

D1729 HOPPER COKE WAGON   Diagram Book Page 13A

Drawing No. 13/1363   **Figure 66**

◀ **Plate 172** This well known photograph shows the pioneer wagon, No. 299900, of lot 552 built by the Birmingham Carriage & Wagon Company Ltd in 1930.

Photograph British Rail

Built to lot numbers 552/879/880.

A total of 200 wagons was built — 100 in 1930 numbered 299900–299999 and 100 in 1935 numbered 699000–699099, and all were built by the trade. No other photographs, apart from **Plate 172,** are known to exist and the author regrets being unable to illustrate vehicles in post-1936 or BR livery.

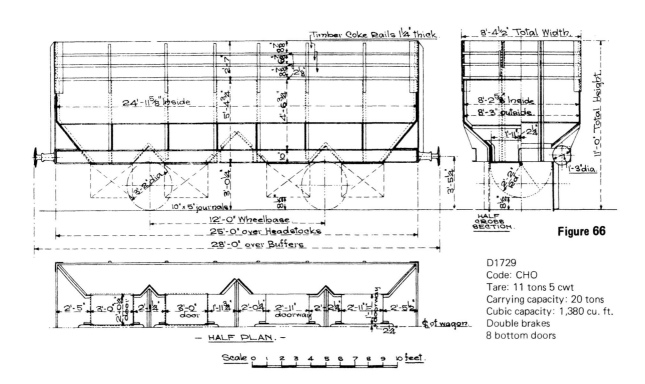

D1729
Code: CHO
Tare: 11 tons 5 cwt
Carrying capacity: 20 tons
Cubic capacity: 1,380 cu. ft.
Double brakes
8 bottom doors

D1800 HOPPER WAGON (BALLAST)

Drawing number not known   **Figure 67**

In 1928 the Leeds Forge built 20 wagons and only one running number is known. Lot 371 covered this construction and a Leeds Forge drawing was used.

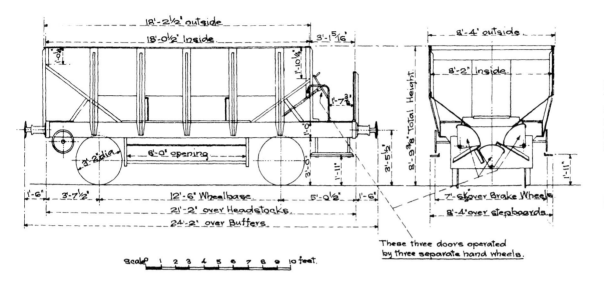

D1800
Tare: 10 tons
Carrying capacity: 25 tons
Cubic capacity: 550 cu. ft.
Screw hand brake
3 bottom doors

Figure 67

Plate 173 This picture of No. 282504 is in ex-works condition and appears to be in light grey livery. In BR days, livery would be similar to that illustrated in **Plate 175.**

Photograph British Rail

D1804 HOPPER WAGON (BALLAST)

Drawing No. 13/1673   **Figure 68**

In 1932 a total of 108 wagons was built to lot 634 by Metropolitan Cammell and were numbered 197272–197379

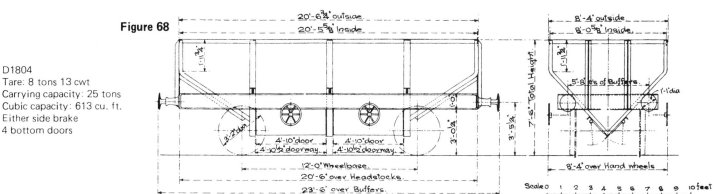

Figure 68

D1804
Tare: 8 tons 13 cwt
Carrying capacity: 25 tons
Cubic capacity: 613 cu. ft.
Either side brake
4 bottom doors

Plate 174

Plate 174 Wagon No. 197273 is shown here in original condition and was allocated to the Western Division.

Photograph British Rail

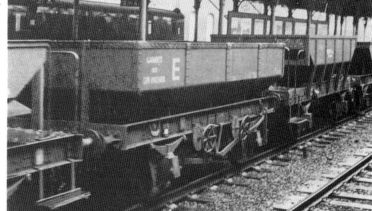

Plate 175 This picture of No. DM197343 taken in 1965 illustrates a vehicle in BR livery.

Photograph Author's Collection

Plate 175

D2024 HOPPER WAGON

Drawing No. 13/2729   **Figure 69**

Derby Works built a total of 450 wagons in 1939 to lot 1199 and these wagons were numbered 697000–697449. They were probably used to carry coal for power stations or heating boilers and, as such, have escaped the attention of photographers, except for the official photograph reproduced as **Plate 176**.

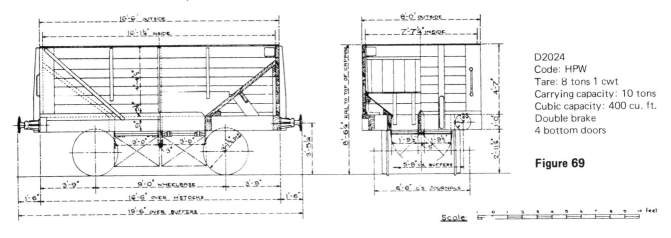

D2024
Code: HPW
Tare: 8 tons 1 cwt
Carrying capacity: 10 tons
Cubic capacity: 400 cu. ft.
Double brake
4 bottom doors

Figure 69

Plate 176 This illustrates wagon No. 697006 in bauxite livery as built and carries a February 1939 paint date. The branding on the bodyside reads 'Crewe Works and Rhigos Colliery, Glyn Neath. G.W.R.'

Photograph British Rail

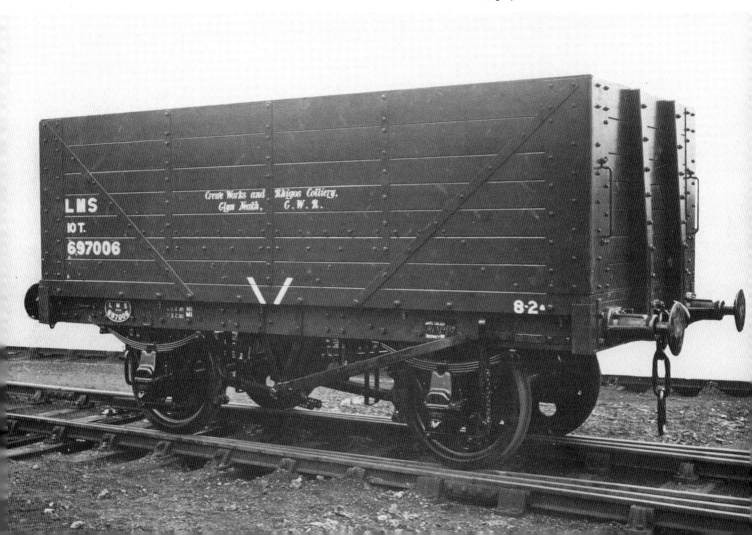

D1669 HOPPER ORE WAGON

Drawing No. 5186 1924 construction
Drawing No. 14/504 1929 construction

Figure 70

Built to lot numbers 74—77/465—468.

200 wagons numbered 299051—299250 were built in 1924 and a further 400 numbered 189571—189970 were constructed in 1929, all by the trade using two separate drawings. Two pictures only are known to exist and these are reproduced as **Plates 177** and **178**. Regrettably, the author cannot be certain about the post-1936 livery style but it is presumed that when painted bauxite the insignia, 'LMS', '20T', and '299063' would be carried in three lines in the panel where the 'L' is located.

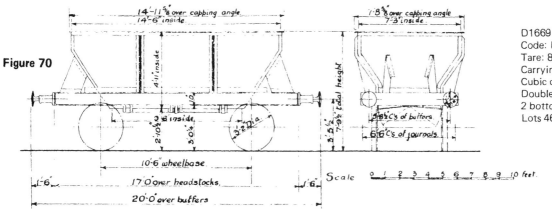

Figure 70

D1669
Code: HPO
Tare: 8 tons 5 cwt
Carrying capacity: 20 tons
Cubic capacity: 363 cu. ft.
Double brake
2 bottom doors
Lots 465, 466, 467, 468

Plate 177

Plate 177 This illustrates No. 299063 of lot 74 built by the Metropolitan Carriage, Wagon and Finance Co. in 1924.
Photograph British Rail

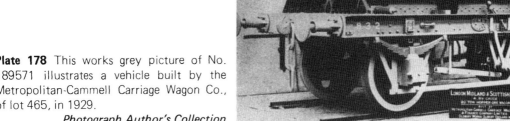

Plate 178 This works grey picture of No. 189571 illustrates a vehicle built by the Metropolitan-Cammell Carriage Wagon Co., of lot 465, in 1929.
Photograph Author's Collection

D1708 HOPPER WAGON (Side Discharge)

Drawing 13/1416   **Figure 71**

Built in 1929 by the Birmingham Carriage & Wagon Co. Ltd to lot 457 and numbered 189301—30, these vehicles were used in block train working from the Toton area to Stonebridge Park power station in North West London, which generated the power for the suburban electric train services of the LMS. They were finally withdrawn c1966 when Stonebridge Park power station was closed.

D1708
Code: LHZ
Tare: 18 tons 15 cwt
Carrying capacity: 40 tons
Load on rail per axle: 14.69 tons
Cubic capacity: 1,794 cu. ft.
Compound lever and AV brakes
4 side doors

Figure 71

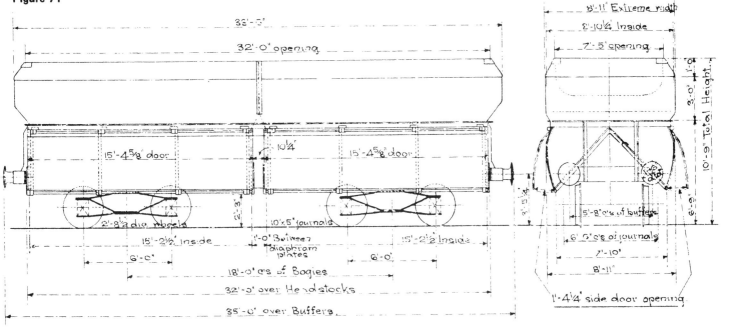

◄ **Plate 179** This illustrates No. 189301 in original ex-works condition.
Photograph British Rail

Plate 180 This picture illustrates No. M189327 at Coalville in 1964 and displays the final livery style carried by these wagons.
Photograph Author's Collection

Plate 180

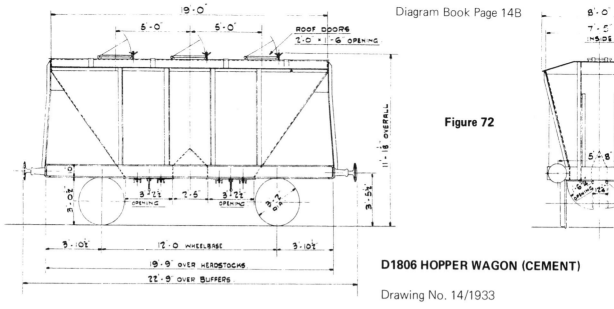

Figure 72

D1806 HOPPER WAGON (CEMENT)

Drawing No. 14/1933

Figure 72

The lot book is not clear as to the quantity built to lot 639 and it is not possible to record any running numbers, apart from the one on the wagon illustrated in **Plate 181.** These wagons were built by the Metropolitan Carriage, Wagon & Finance Company in 1932 and it is interesting to note that, although the diagram states they were fitted with double brakes, the photograph of No. 299894 indicates that at least one was equipped with Morton-type brakes but with shoes on each wheel.

Photograph British Rail

D1806
Code: HPO
Tare: 10 tons 18 cwt
Carrying capacity: 20 tons
Double brake
Metal body
3 top doors, 4 bottom doors

Plate 181

D1894 HOPPER WAGON (ORE) Built from Mild Steel

Drawing No. 14/2284   **Figure 73**

Built to lot numbers 790/866/867
Identical to D1893 apart from the type of steel used.

300 wagons were built by the trade during 1934 and were numbered 690050–690349. Regrettably, they do not appear to have been officially photographed but their early livery condition would have been similar to wagon No. 690000, **Plate 183.**

Plate 182 This illustrates wagon No. M690335, uprated to 21T and branded for limestone traffic, in 1965.

Photograph D. P. Rowland

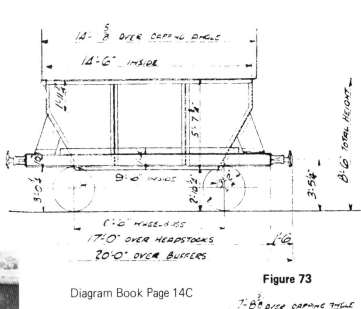

Figure 73

Diagram Book Page 14C

D1894
Code: HPO
Tare: 8 tons 6 cwt
Carrying capacity: 20 tons
Cubic capacity: 430 cu. ft.
Double brake
2 bottom doors
Lots 790, 866, 867

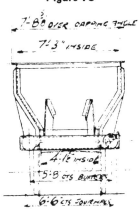

SCALE

0 1 2 3 4 5 6 7 8 9 10 FEET.

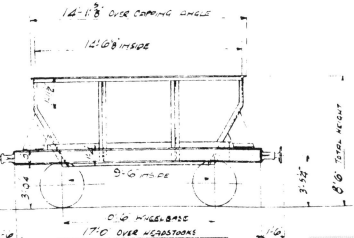

Figure 74

D1893
Code: HPO
Tare: 7 tons 16 cwt
Carrying capacity: 20 tons
Cubic capacity: 430 cu. ft.
Double brake
2 bottom doors
Chromador steel
Lot 783

SCALE

0 1 2 3 4 5 6 7 8 9 10
FEET.

D1893 HOPPER WAGON (ORE) Built from Chromador Steel

Diagram Book Page 14D

Drawing No. 14/2306   **Figure 74**

Identical to D1894 apart from the type of steel used.

In 1934 50 wagons numbered 690000–690049 were built to lot 789 by the Metropolitan Carriage, Wagon & Finance Company Ltd. and appear to have been identical to page 14C apart from the type of steel used in their construction as noted upon the diagrams.

Plate 183 This illustrates No. 690000 when first built.

Photograph British Rail

D1941 HOPPER WAGON (ORE) Built from Copper Bearing Steel

Drawing No. 14/2284A   **Figure 75**

Built to lot numbers 940/941/966/967/1020/1133/1134.

During the period 1936–38 a total of 450 wagons were built by the trade to lots noted above. It will have been seen that the LMS were experimenting with different grades of steel for wagon construction (see pages 14C and 14D) and again D1941/2, pages 14E/14F appear to be identical vehicles but were probably constructed from varying grades, this diagram specifying copper bearing steel. Running numbers were: 690350–690899, 691000–691899.

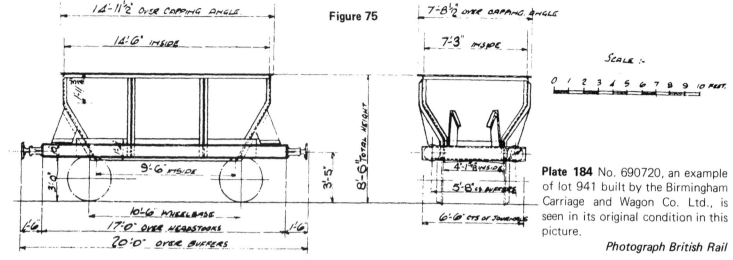

Figure 75

Plate 184 No. 690720, an example of lot 941 built by the Birmingham Carriage and Wagon Co. Ltd., is seen in its original condition in this picture.

Photograph British Rail

Plate 184

Plate 185 This picture of No. 691576 shows an example of lot 1133, built in 1938, as running in 1964.

Photograph J. Johnson

Plate 185

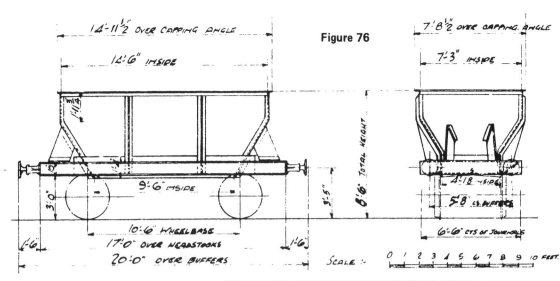

Figure 76

D1942
Code: HPO
Tare:
Carrying capacity: 20 tons
Cubic capacity: 430 cu. ft.
Double brake
2 bottom doors

D1942 HOPPER WAGON (ORE)

Drawing No. 14/2284 **Figure 76**

In 1936 100 vehicles numbered 690900—690999 were constructed by the Gloucester Carriage & Wagon Company to lot 942 and it is possible that this single lot was built for comparative purposes with the copper bearing steel vehicles of D1941, even though the diagram does not specify the material used.

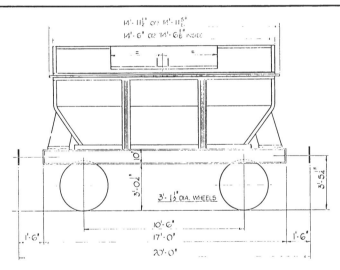

Figure 77

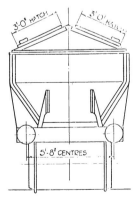

D2194
Top doors to be centrally situated and open into a 7' 6'' hatch
2 bottom doors
Converted from LMS freight stock diagrams 14C, 14D, 14E

Plate 185A This picture of No. 690951 is the Gloucester Railway Carriage & Wagon Company official picture and no other illustrations of vehicles from this batch are known to the author.
Photograph OPC Collection

D2194 HOPPER WAGON (LIME) Diagram Book Page 14G

Drawing number for modification not known **Figure 77**

It will be seen from the diagram that these vehicles were conversions from pages 14C, 14D and 14E but no reference to these conversions appear in the lot book so the author is unable to say how many were converted or what their running numbers were.

Plate 186 This is the only picture known to the author and the number is M691141. As noted on the diagram, the conversion was a peak roof with a hatch for loading purposes.
Photograph D. Larkin

D1670 MEAT VAN

Drawing 6630 lot 306   **Figure 78**
       13/796 lot 480

A total of 400 vans was built to D1670, 300 at Wolverton to lot 306 in 1927 and 100 in 1930 to lot 480.

Regrettably, it is not known how many were through pipe only and how many were fitted with vacuum brakes. Nevertheless, three pictures exist, all showing different liveries and these are reproduced in **Plates 187—189**. In addition to the numbers quoted in the plates, one other number, 171331, has been noted. Known running numbers: 171271, 173127, 258353, 258360, 267107.

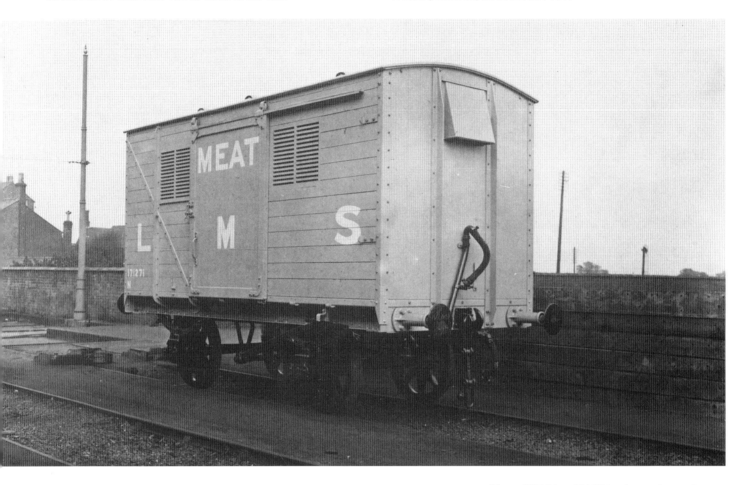

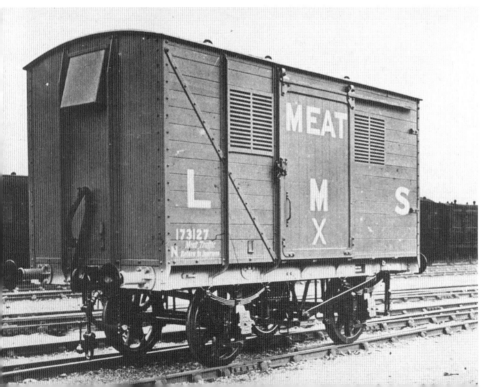

Plate 187 No. 171271, shown here, should be compared with No. 173127 **(Plate 188),** which displays an entirely different layout for the livery. From the solebar paint date, No. 171271 was part of lot 306 and so would be carrying the earlier style. From the same batch, Nos. 258353 and 258360 have also been recorded.

Photographs British Rail

Plate 188

D1670
Code: MV
Tares,   hand brake and through pipe:
          8 tons 6 cwt
          fully fitted: 8 tons 13 cwt 2 qrs
Carrying capacity: 6 tons, passenger
                    8 tons, goods
'Morton' brake
All fitted with steam train pipe
Sliding door on each side

Scale

0 1 2 3 4 5 6 7 8 9 10 feet.

17'-6' outside
17'-3½' inside
5'-0' doorway
Side Vent Perf'd Zinc
Decoli's floor
End Ventilators
7'-8¼' inside
9'-0' wheelbase
17'-6' over Headstocks
20'-11' over buffers
3'-1½' dia
4'-1' rail to floor
3'-5¼'
1'-8½'
1'-8½'

8'-1' over side stanchions.
8'-1¼' over sliding doors
7'-2½' between cant rails.
3'-10'
7'-5¾' inside
8'-4' over door fastenings
8'-4½' over commode handles
11'-10½' Rail to top of Roof
12'-0¾' total height
5'-8' c's of buffers
6'-6' c's of journals

Figure 78

Plate 189 This illustrates No. M267107 photographed in 1949 when painted in bauxite. Note the train steam heating pipes, also visible on **Plate 187,** for use when coupled between the locomotive and the coaches whilst running in passenger trains.

Photograph British Rail   **Plate 189**

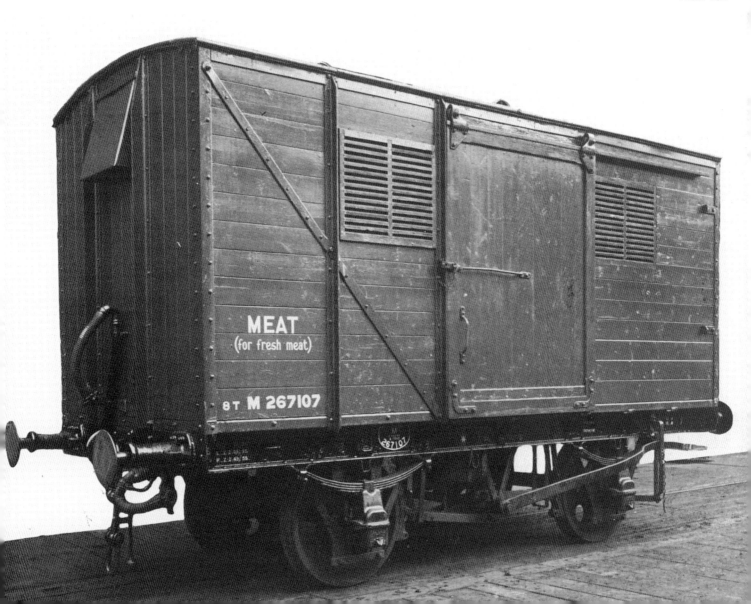

MEAT
(for fresh meat)

8 T M 267107

D1821 MEAT VAN

Diagram Book Page 15A

Drawing No. 13/1468 **Figure 79**

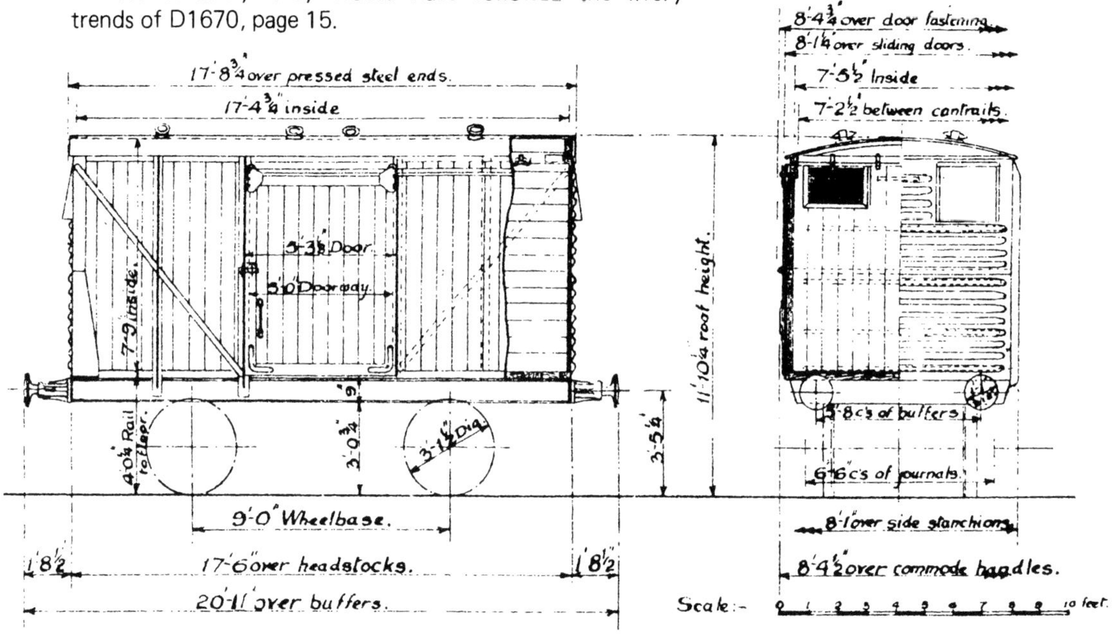

D1821
Code: MV
Tare: 8 tons 10 cwt 1 qr
Carrying capacity: 6 tons
AV and hand brakes
Sliding door on each side
Lot 497

Lot 497 built in 1930 at Derby was for a total of 66 vehicles using random running numbers. Unlike the vehicles built to D1670, page 15, these vans were built with corrugated steel ends. No pictures are known to exist and it is therefore impossible to give any running numbers. Almost certainly they would have followed the livery trends of D1670, page 15.

Figure 79

D1822 VENTILATED MEAT VAN

Diagram Book Page 15B

Drawing No. 13/1394 **Figure 80**

D1822
Code: MV
Tare: 9 tons 2 cwt 3 qrs
Carrying capacity: 6 tons
AV and hand brakes
Sliding door on each side
Lot 498

Lot 498 was for a total of 34 vehicles built at Derby in 1930 and, unlike the previous batch, these vans ran on 3'6½" diameter wheels on a 10'0" wheelbase. Again, no pictures of these are known to exist and their absence makes it impossible to give any running numbers or to confirm the livery trends. However, the pictures on page 15 probably apply to page 15B, in so far as a general lay-out was concerned.

Figure 80

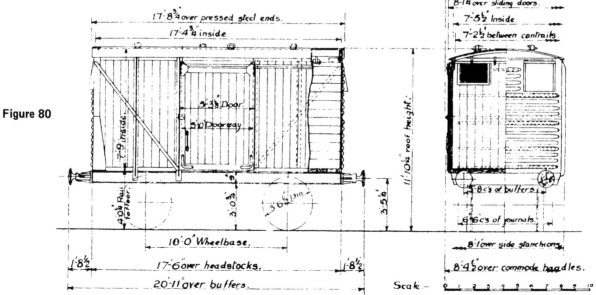

D1671 STANDARD MINERAL WAGON (END DOOR)

Classified by BR as End Door Wagon

Drawing No. RCH STD 1002 up to lot 172   **Figure 81**
             6467 from lot 254
             13/2044 from lot 830

Built to lot numbers 40—55/59/108/118/162—172/254—267/ 294/324/330/347/380/383/386/422/494/830—832/915—917/ 1006/1021/1022/1108/1109/1206.

A very large quantity of wagons were built to this diagram during the period 1924—1940 and the early construction up to 1930 was divided between the trade and Earlestown. By that year, a total of 22,251 vehicles had been built, carrying random numbers, and the following have been recorded: 45605, 60975, 108203, 171253, 179653, 228077, 242176, 256180, 268985, 315512, 324252, 322789, 333287, 350592, 351270.

In 1935, further construction began at Derby and, by 1940, a further 8,546 were produced carrying running numbers 600000—607000 and 608000—609545. It is not entirely clear why there was a gap in the numbers between 607001—607999. A number of pictures have been selected to illustrate the various livery styles which briefly can be summarized as: grey with large letters 'LMS', grey with small 'LMS', and bauxite with small 'LMS'. As far as can be seen the large grey letters ended around wagon No. 603999 and there was then a batch of grey wagons with small 'LMS' (**Plate 196**), but by wagon No. 605000, they were probably being turned out in bauxite. All these were 12T capacity but, by about No. 609000, they were uprated to 13T (see **Plate 198**).

Plate 190

Plates 190 and **191** These two pictures illustrate wagon No. 351270 built by the Gloucester Railway Carriage and Wagon Co. Ltd in August 1924 and, apart from being good pictures from a detail and livery standpoint, they clearly indicate that the white stripe had not yet been introduced (see **Plate 192**).

Photographs Gloucester Carriage & Wagon Co. Ltd

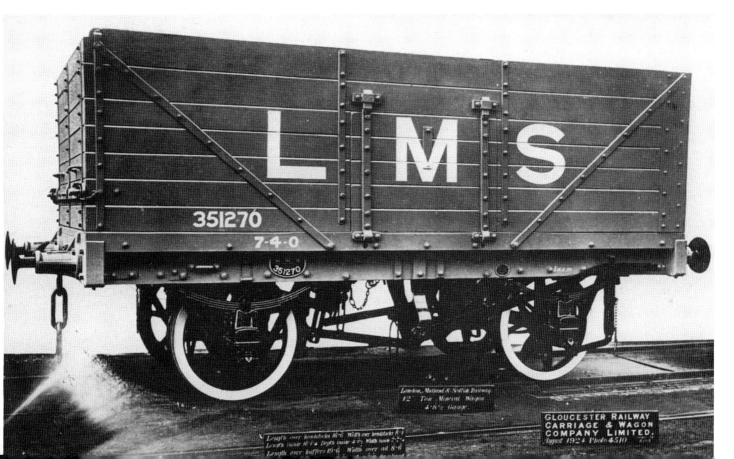

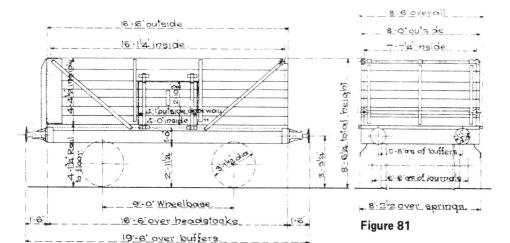

Figure 81

D1671
Code: EDW
Tare: 7 tons
Carrying capacity: 12 tons
Cubic capacity: 534 cu. ft.
Double brake
2 side doors, 2 bottom doors, 1 end door

Scale 0 1 2 3 4 5 6 7 8 9 10 feet

Plate 192 This illustrates wagon No. 33328 and, apart from the stripe being different from Plate 194, the wagon has disc wheels.
Photograph W. Hudson Collection

Plate 193 No. 228077 was built at Earlestown in 1928 and this picture has been included to show the correct method of loading barrels in open wagons and to illustrate the bottom doors which can just be seen through the open doorway. These bottom doors were indicated by the stripes but the date of their introduction is not known.
Photograph British Rail

Plate 194

Plate 194 This illustrates wagon No. 60975 built by the Derbyshire Carriage and Wagon Company Ltd. Note the method of painting the white stripe when compared with other plates. The purpose of this stripe was to indicate clearly that the end door was at the high end of the stripe.

Photograph Author's Collection

Plate 195 Wagon No. 602604 is seen in the grey livery style in use just prior to the change to small letters, which preceded the change in body colour from grey to bauxite.

Photograph British Rail

Plate 195

Plate 196 No. 604889, photographed in 1939, is in grey livery with the small size 'LMS' but still with the large stripe which was soon to be reduced in size.
Photograph A. E. West

Plate 196

Plate 197 This picture of No. 605796, part of lot 1021, shows a wagon in bauxite body colour with the correct size insignia and bottom door markings but displaying the large white strip more usually associated with the grey liveried wagons.

Photograph British Rail

Plate 198 No. 609525 displays the correct insignia style in bauxite but this vehicle was rated at 13T when built.

Photograph British Rail

Plate 198

Plate 199

Plate 199 This picture of wagon No. M603289 has been included to illustrate the final BR livery style of unpainted wood, rusty ironwork, white \ / markings to indicate hopper bottom, and end door stripe painted on diagonal strapping. Note the legend 'COND 28.9.63' and the stencil marking 'One journey only, loco coal'.

Photograph Author's Collection

D2049 13 TON MERCHANDISE WAGON

Figure 82

No drawing appears to have been issued to cover this modification to convert mineral wagons to merchandise wagons and, according to the diagram, 100 vehicles were converted c1946, although there is some evidence to suggest that the total was higher. No official pictures were taken and the only photograph available to the author is depicted in **Plate 200**. No. 85299 is the only known running number of an LMS built vehicle which was converted, similar conversions being made to L N E R and Private Owner 7 plank mineral wagons.

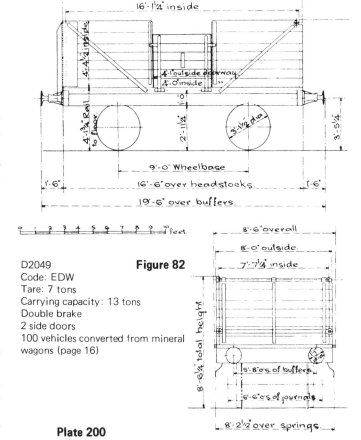

D2049
Code: EDW
Tare: 7 tons
Carrying capacity: 13 tons
Double brake
2 side doors
100 vehicles converted from mineral wagons (page 16)

Plate 200 This illustrates wagon No. 85299 at Wimbledon when it was involved in an accident. It is not known if the vehicle was repaired or scrapped. Note the branding 'not to be used for coal traffic'. If repainted when converted, bauxite would be the livery employed so possibly they were returned to traffic without being so treated.

Photograph S. C. Townroe

Plate 200

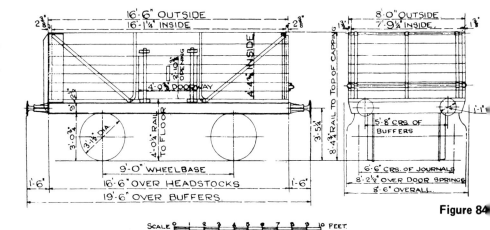

Figure 83

D2061
Code: EDW
Tare: 7 tons
Carrying capacity: 13 tons
Cubic capacity: 534 cu. ft.
Double brake
2 side doors, 2 bottom doors, 1 end door

D2102   Diagram Book Page 16C
Code: EDW
Tare: 7 tons 6 cwt
Carrying capacity: 13 tons
Cubic capacity: 547 cu. ft.
Double brake
2 side doors, 2 bottom doors, 1 end door

D2061 END DOOR WAGON

Drawing No. 6467   **Figure**
Lot 384/5

200 vehicles were built at Earlestown
1928 to the same drawing number as t
wooden underframe wagons, being built
the same time, and the reason why just 2
with steel underframes were so completed
not known.

No official pictures were taken and
pictures are known to the author and, sin
random running numbers were employe
there are, regrettably, no examples record
to assist modellers. Livery would be identi
to the contemporary D1671 wagons.

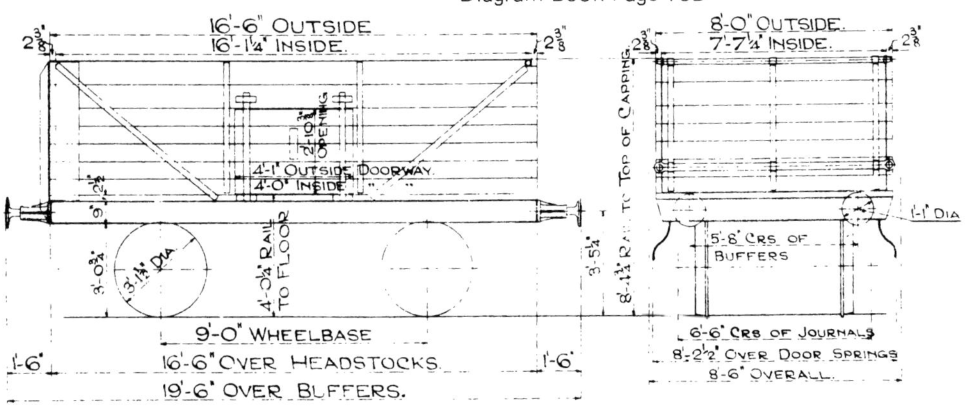

It is interesting to note that these 2
wagons were originally allocated to D16
and it was not until many years later th
they were separated and given their ov
diagram number.

D2102 END DOOR WAGON

Drawing No. 13/3576   **Figure 84**

Built to lot numbers 1368–1370/1379/
1386.

The 5,500 wagons built from 1946
onwards and numbered 609546–615045
were the final examples of wooden bodied
mineral wagons with steel underframes to be
built by the LMS. They, in common with all
wartime and immediate post-war wooden
vehicles, were built with thinner planks
which gave slightly wider internal
measurements.

Figure 84

SCALE [FEET]

Plate 201 Wagon No. 610803 carried the 'unpainted' livery
employed when these vehicles were built and the wooden parts of
many vehicles were probably never painted during their lifetime.
Photograph British Rail

Plate 202 This picture of wagon No. M610973 in its final days
service during 1964. Note the 'One journey only, loco coal' brandi
Photograph Author's Collecti

D2106 END DOOR WAGON

Drawing No. 13/3665 **Figure 85**

One wagon only, No. 616000 to lot 1412 was built at Derby in 1945 as the prototype of the familiar 16 ton steel bodied mineral wagons.

D2106
Code: END
Tare: 7 tons 15 cwt
Carrying capacity: 16 tons
Cubic capacity: 626 cu. ft.
Double brake
2 side doors, 2 bottom doors, 1 end door

16' 9" OUTSIDE
16' 5½" INSIDE
4' 1" DOORWAY
2' 10"
3' 1½" DIA
9' 0" WHEELBASE
16' 6" OVER HEADSTOCKS
1' 6'
19' 6" OVER BUFFERS
3' 0½"
3' 5"
8' 7⅞" OVERALL

8' 7" OUTSIDE
7' 11½" INSIDE
5' 8" CENTRES BUFFERS
6' 6" CRS OF JOURNALS
8' 4½" OVER DOOR SPRINGS

Figure 85

Diagram Book Page 16D

SCALE 0 1 2 3 4 5 6 7 8 9 10 FEET

Plate 203

Plates **203, 204** and **205** are three official views of this wagon when first built and painted in bauxite livery.

Photographs British Rail

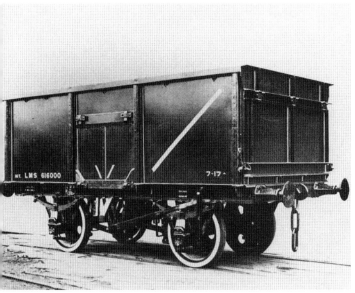

Plate 204

Plate 205

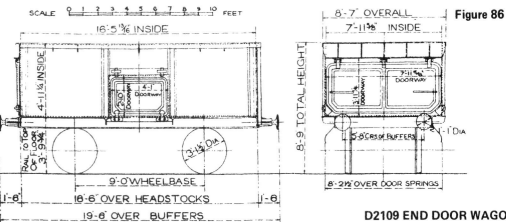

D2109
Code: EDW
Tare: 7 tons 10 cwt
Carrying capacity: 15 tons to 16 tons
Cubic capacity: 648 cu. ft.
Double brake
2 side doors, 2 bottom doors, 1 end door

Plate 206

D2109 END DOOR WAGON

Drawing No. 13/3693 Body   **Figure 86**
13/3694 U/Frame

Built to lot numbers 1415/1468.

Numbered between 616001—618599 these 2,599 vehicles were recorded as being built in 1947 but the evidence of the solebar paint dates suggests that many were produced in 1946 and, in view of the detail differences noted, a number of pictures have been used to illustrate this type of wagon.

Plate 206 Wagon No. 616090 seen in this view in ex-works condition, has the side door depicted on the diagram. Compare with **Plates 207** and **211**.

Photograph British Rail

Plates 207 and **208** both illustrate wagon No. 616955 and attention is drawn to the side and end doors which are different to the other vehicles illustrated and allocated to the diagram. Almost certainly, steel shortages and supply problems led to these variations being employed to complete wagons quickly and get them into traffic.

Photographs British Rail

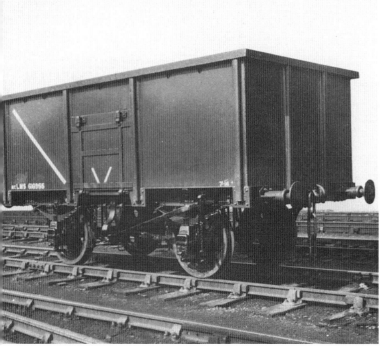

Plate 207   **Plate 208**

Plate 209

Plate 209 This picture of wagon No. 616731 shows both side and end doors as the diagram and the solebar paint date reads '21.1.47' which seems to confirm that some vehicles were built the previous year.

Photograph British Rail

Plate 210 This shows wagon No. M616285 as running in 1964. Compare the end door construction with the diagram and **Plate 208.**

Photograph Author's Collection

Plate 210

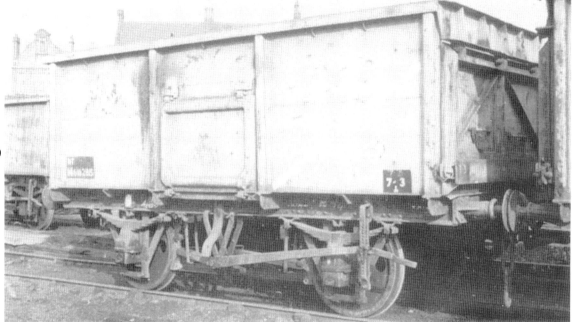

Plate 211 This final picture has been included to show that steel wagons could run with the old open spoke wheels which wagon No. M617643 has obtained prior to being photographed in 1964.

Photograph Author's Collection

Plate 211   109

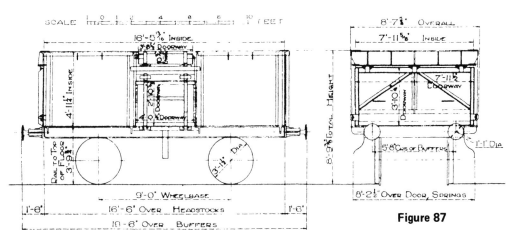

Plate 212

Figure 87

D2134
Code:
Tare: 7 tons 15 cwt
Cubic capacity: 648 cu. ft.
Double brake
2 side doors, 2 flap doors, 2 bottom doors,
1 end door

Diagram Book Page 16F

D2134 16 TON END DOOR WAGON

Drawing No. 13/3750   **Figure 87**
              13/3961

Built to lot numbers 1516/1540
Built in 1949 by British Railways
and numbered M618600—622099
these 3,500 steel wagons formed the
final batch of 16 ton steel mineral
wagons built and allocated to LMS
diagram numbers and the two photographs used to illustrate these vehicles
will show detail differences of welded
and riveted construction.

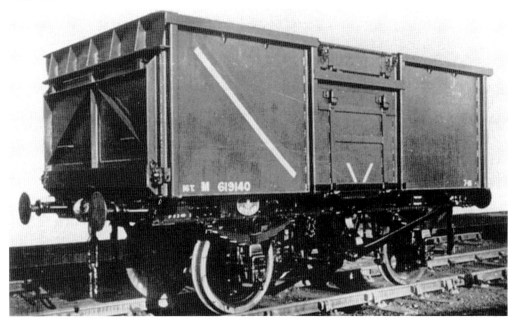

Plate 212 illustrates wagon No.
M619140 and it should be compared
with wagon No. 620623 in **Plate 213**.
Particular attention should be paid to
the end and side door construction on
these two vehicles.

Photographs British Rail

D1672 REFRIGERATOR VAN

Drawing No. 5644
Lots 5, 38, 137, 295, 451 - total 450 vehicles

Figure 88

Drawing No. 6496
Lots 203, 414, 499, 500 - total 300 vehicles

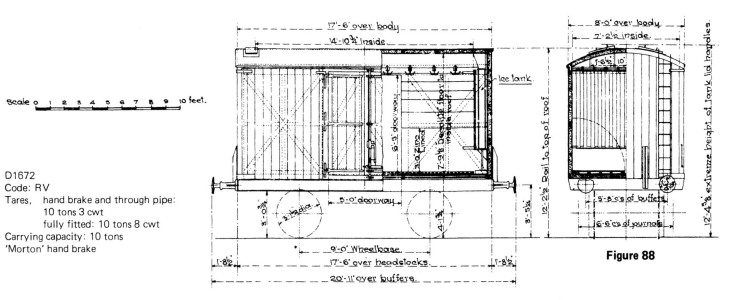

D1672
Code: RV
Tares, hand brake and through pipe:
    10 tons 3 cwt
    fully fitted: 10 tons 8 cwt
Carrying capacity: 10 tons
'Morton' hand brake

Figure 88

D1672A INSULATED MEAT VAN

(Supersedes D1672)

Figure 89

The history of these vehicles is somewhat confusing and, in particular, the use of two separate drawing numbers interspersed between the lots is difficult to understand.

When originally constructed, they were fitted with tanks filled with ice, which melted during the course of the journey, but later, the development of 'dry ice' (solid carbon dioxide) rendered these tanks obsolete and so the tanks and ladders were removed and a new diagram was issued to cover this amendment. For this reason, the two diagrams have been considered together.

In 1936, there was a scheme to modify 100 vans for banana traffic but it is not possible to state if this scheme was carried through. Known running numbers: 7703, 189544, 264756.

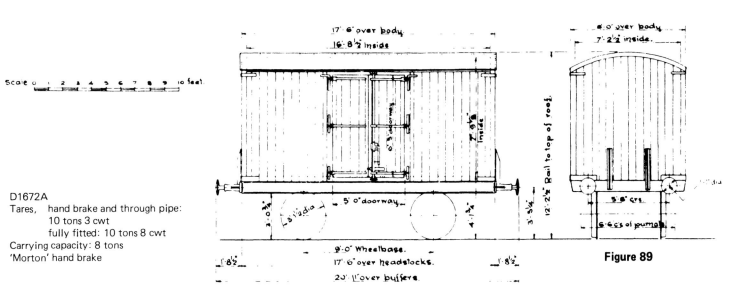

D1672A
Tares, hand brake and through pipe:
    10 tons 3 cwt
    fully fitted: 10 tons 8 cwt
Carrying capacity: 8 tons
'Morton' hand brake

Figure 89

Plate 214

Plate 214 This picture illustrates van No. 7703 when first built and allocated to D1672. Note the top of the ladder, visible at the left hand end. When photographed, no 'N' was displayed and there appears to be no evidence of special branding in respect of passenger or goods train loading mentioned on the diagram.

Photograph British Rail

Plate 215

Plate 215 This picture of van No 264756 carrying a '19.1.33' paint date and a 'Built 1926 Derby' plate shows a conversion to D1672A with the ice tanks removed but still retaining the end ladder. It should also be noted that No. 264756 is a 'through pipe' vehicle and should be compared with **Plate 214** illustrating van No. 7703.

Plate 216 This early British Railways picture of M189544 shows the livery style used during their final period of ownership. It is not known just how they were liveried in the post-1936 period after the change to bauxite had been agreed for most stock. Prior to 1936 grey was the body colour but this BR picture suggests that a white body colour was used.

Photograph Author's Collection

Diagram Book Page 18

D1673 VENTILATED REFRIGERATOR VAN

Drawing No. 6429   **Figure 90**

A total of 30 vehicles built to lot 133 at Derby in 1927/8 were allocated to this diagram and generally were very similar to D1672. However, in due course they were trans-ferred to the Non-Passenger Coaching Stock book and re-allocated to D1883. Later, as with D1672, they were amended to D1883A and, in due course, the 1934 coaching stock renumbering allocated them to 38700–38729.

No pictures are known to exist showing these vehicles in either their original form or later in the livery of non-passenger coaching stock.

D1673   **Figure 90**
Code: VRV
Tare: 10 tons 10 cwt
Carrying capacity: 6 tons
'Morton' brake
Door on each side

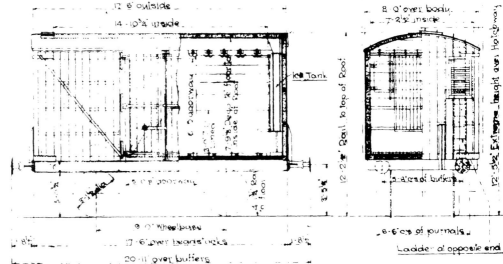

113

D1674 DOUBLE BOLSTER WAGON

Drawing No. 6105 **Figure 91**
Built to lot numbers 209–211/277/278/391

Drawing No. 14/1181 Lot 534

Known running numbers: 231331, 235329, 263301, 286040, 289483, 300742, 302191, 315583, 317842, 325110.

This diagram totals 1,411 vehicles built both by the trade and railway works between 1925 and 1930. These vehicles were used for the carriage of long loads and, when first built, displayed variations of livery styles as shown in the plates.

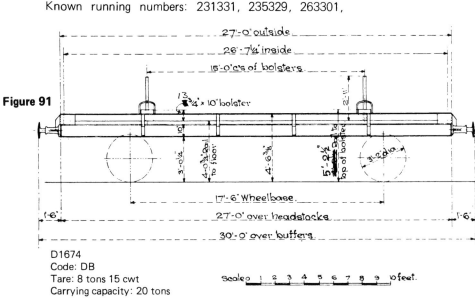

Figure 91

D1674
Code: DB
Tare: 8 tons 15 cwt
Carrying capacity: 20 tons
'Morton' brake

Plate 217

Plate 219 This illustrates a conversion of a double bolster wagon No. M321371 to a canopy wagon for carrying pipes. The exact date of this conversion is not known and could have been pre-1948 as the branding reads 'When empty return to Staveley Works, Nr. Chesterfield, LMS or LNE Railways'.

Photograph British Rail

Plate 217 Wagon No. 263301 in original condition.

Photograph British Rail

Plate 218 Wagon No. 231331 built by the Gloucester Carriage & Wagon Co. Ltd and the location of the running numbers, 'LMS' etc should be compared with wagon No. 263301 in **Plate 217.**

Photograph Gloucester Carriage & Wagon Co. Ltd

Plate 219

Plate 220

Plate 220 This 1962 picture of M289483 shows a D1674 wagon uprated to 22T, as indeed was M321371 in **Plate 219**. Note replacement axleboxes.

Photograph D. P. Rowland

Plate 221 No. 286040, as running in 1964, displays the unpainted livery style of British Railways for wooden bodied vehicles during the 1950s and 1960s.

Photograph Author's Collection

Plate 221

Plate 222

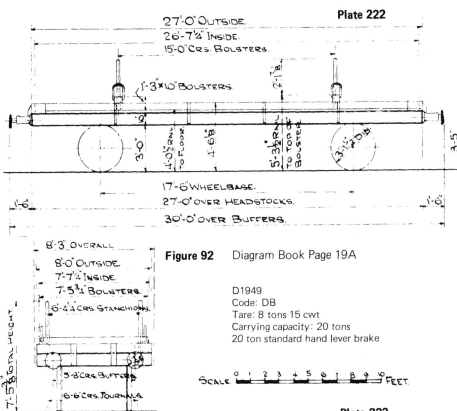

27'-0" OUTSIDE.
26'-7½" INSIDE.
15'-0" CRS. BOLSTERS.

1'-3"×10" BOLSTERS.

17'-6" WHEELBASE.
27'-0" OVER HEADSTOCKS.
30'-0" OVER BUFFERS.

8'-3" OVERALL
8'-0" OUTSIDE.
7'-7¼" INSIDE.
7'-5¾" BOLSTERS.
6'-4¼" CRS STANCHIONS.

7'-5⅝" TOTAL HEIGHT.

5'-8" CRS BUFFERS.
6'-6" CRS JOURNALS.

Figure 92 Diagram Book Page 19A

D1949
Code: DB
Tare: 8 tons 15 cwt
Carrying capacity: 20 tons
20 ton standard hand lever brake

SCALE 0 1 2 3 4 5 6 7 8 9 6 FEET.

D1949 DOUBLE BOLSTER WAGON

Drawing No. 13/2332 **Figure 92**

Built to lot numbers 969/980 – 982/1139 – 1141.

Carrying running numbers 725000–725799, these 800 wagons built between 1936 and 1938 carried three livery styles when first constructed.

The Derby built vehicles 725000–725149 were all liveried as **Plate 222** which shows No. 725128 in original condition and carrying a '7.8.36' paint date. This is a clear example of the post-1936 insignia style with the grey body colour.

Photograph British Rail

Plate 223 A Charles Roberts vehicle No. 725560 in 1936 and part of a lot numbered 725350–725549. Note the central close-spaced 'LMS' and large 'DOUBLE'. The white tyres were probably for photographic purposes.

Photograph British Rail

Plate 223

Plate 224

Plate 224 This illustrates wagon No. 725005, in service as a runner to ex-Midland 8 ton low goods wagon No. 3600. There appears to be a problem with the load!

Photograph British Rail

Plate 225

Plate 225 This picture of No. 725740 shows the first of a 1938 batch built by Charles Roberts and displays the correct post-1936 insignia style with a bauxite body colour.

Photograph National Railway Museum

Plate 226

Plate 226 This final picture has been included to illustrate a load chained on to a double bolster whose running number cannot be seen.

Photograph Author's Collection

D2029 DOUBLE BOLSTER

Diagram Book Page 19B

Drawing No. 6637

Figure 93

The lot book records 201 Derby-built vehicles to lots 313 and 315 which, from their position in the diagram book, would seem to have originally carried another diagram number and to ha[ve] been located elsewhere, since it is difficult to see how, with t[he] logical system employed by the LMS, these vehicles, built [in] 1927, could have followed the 1936 construction of page 19[A].

They carried random numbers and only three examples a[re] known: 41683, 125088, 150257.

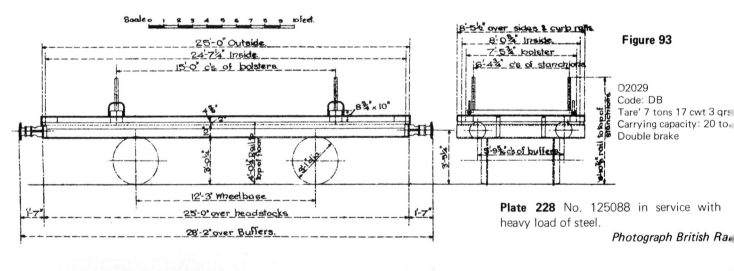

Figure 93

D2029
Code: DB
Tare' 7 tons 17 cwt 3 qrs
Carrying capacity: 20 to[ns]
Double brake

Plate 228 No. 125088 in service with heavy load of steel.

Photograph British Ra[il]

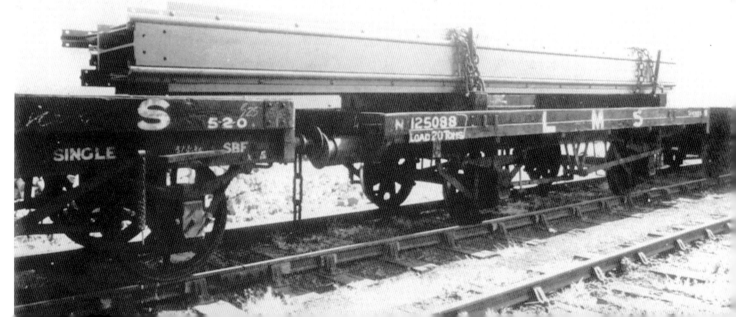

D2050 TWIN BOLSTER WAGON   Diagram Book Page 19C

No drawing number appears to have been issued   **Figure 94**

In October 1940 it was reported that heavy imports of iron and steel were expected for the duration of the war with peak tonnages of 850,000 tons per month. Double bolster wagons would be needed to handle this traffic and so it was felt that there would be a shortage of similar wagons for timber traffic. As a result it was suggested that 2,000 mineral wagons could be converted into 1,000 twin bolster sets at a cost of £44.00 per twin set. It was agreed that in the first batch the GWR would convert 90 pairs, the LNER 320 pairs, the SR 90 pairs and the LMS 500 pairs.

The files then contain considerable details, too much to reproduce in this volume but what is clear is that 4,000 'British Railways' owned mineral wagons were converted to 2,000 twin bolsters. Of these, 500 were reconverted to coal wagons in 1945, 346 were converted to twin case wagons in 1942, and 154 were converted into 308 flat case wagons in 1942. 1 was scrapped leaving 999 as twin bolsters after 1945. Vehicles of LMS, LNER, and private owner origin were converted, probably on a 'first come first served' basis.

No pictures are known and no running numbers have been recorded.

D2050
Code: TB
Tare: 8 tons 0 cwt (average for each wagon)
Carrying capacity: 24 tons to 26 tons according to tare and age of wagons
Length of load not to exceed 33'0''
Double brake

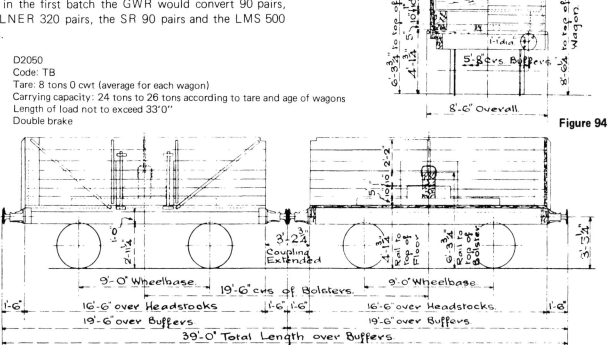

Figure 94

D2067 20 TON DOUBLE BOLSTER TRUCK

Drawing No. 13/3418   **Figure 95**

Built at Derby and Wolverton to lot 1315 and totalling 200 vehicles numbered 725800–725999, these wagons were very similar to the previous construction and while no pictures showing their original condition are known to exist they probably entered traffic with the wooden parts unpainted.

Diagram Book Page 19D

D2067
Code: Double
Tare: 10 tons 15 cwt
Carrying capacity: 20 tons
20 ton standard hand lever brake
Bolsters and stanchions removable

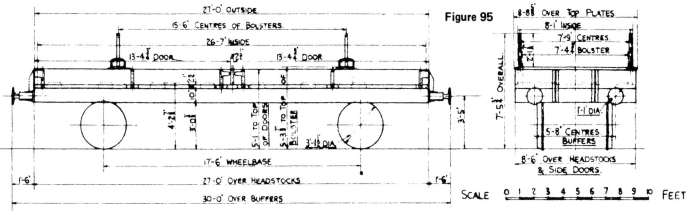

Figure 95

Plate 229 This illustrates wagon No. M725860 at Horwich in 1965.

Photograph Author's Collection

D2077 TWIN BOLSTER WAGON

Diagram Book Page 19E

No drawing appears to have been issued

Figure 96

This diagram was another wartime conversion from D1671 mineral wagons which had already been converted to twin bolster wagons. This saw the removal of the sides and ends, together with the removal of the buffers at the inner ends to enable permanent couplings to be fitted. It is recorded that 171 pairs were so altered and examples are shown in **Plates 231, 232** and **233** and the running numbers have been recorded. The full story is related on page 19C, D2050.

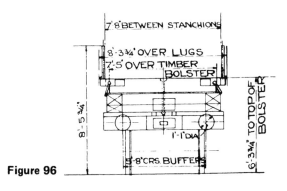

Figure 96

D2077
Code: Twincase
Tare: 12 tons 8 cwt (the pair)
Carrying capacity: 18 tons (the pair)
Double brake

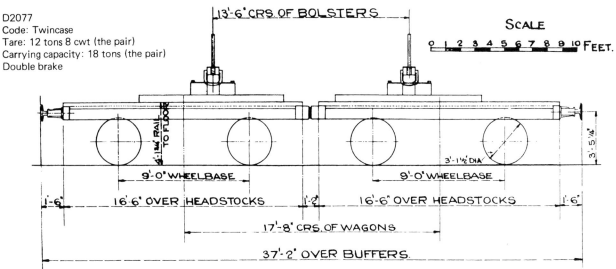

Plate 230

Plate 231

Plates 230, 231 and **232** These three pictures illustrate Nos. M315810 and M600828 taken at Peterborough in September 1953 and are the only pictures of these vehicles known to the author. **Plate 230** shows the pair, **Plate 231** is a close up of M315810, and **Plate 232** shows how the bolster is made up.

Photographs A. E. West

Plate 232

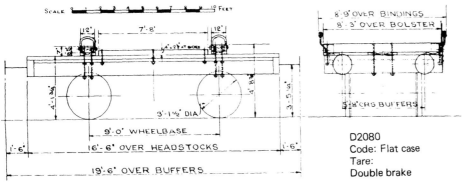

Figure 97

D2080
Code: Flat case
Tare:
Double brake

D2080 FLAT CASE WAGON

No drawing appears to have been issued   **Figure 97**

A further conversion, recorded as totalling 146 vehicles, saw the removal of the sides and ends of D1671 mineral wagons in 1942/3. Again, no official pictures are known to exist and no running numbers have been recorded. The full story appears on page 19C.

Diagram Book Page 19F

Plate 233 The only picture of a flat case wagon conversion found by the author. Its mineral wagon origin can be seen by the shape of the buffers. It is not known from which batch No. 72156 came, it carries an LMS repair plate dated 1937 and the legend 'PE GW 23.10.42'.

Photograph British Rail/OPC

D2105 21 TON DOUBLE BOLSTER WAGON

Drawing No. 12/691   **Figure 98**

Diagram Book Page 19G

Built to lot numbers 1384/1414/1458/1525/1536

Built between 1945 and 1949 and numbered 726000–727049, these 1,050 wagons saw the change from wooden to steel construction for double bolster wagons. The batch up to about No. 726399 probably all came out in bauxite livery lettered 'LMS' but later vehicles would have had the running number prefixed 'M' but painted in the light grey adopted by British Railways.

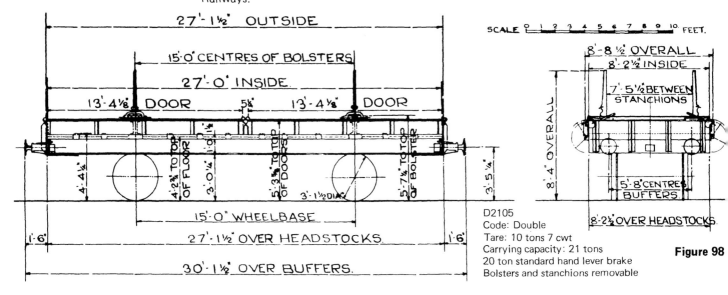

D2105
Code: Double
Tare: 10 tons 7 cwt
Carrying capacity: 21 tons
20 ton standard hand lever brake
Bolsters and stanchions removable

Figure 98

Plate 234 This illustrates wagon No. 726018 in original condition.

Photograph British Rail

Plate 235 Photographed in 1965 No. M726954 is now branded 'Plate' and has had the bolsters removed.

Photograph Author's Collection

Plate 236 A number of these vehicles were modified to trestle plate wagons and this picture shows No. M727044 as running in 1964 with a 21 ton capacity in this modified condition. Other vehicles so converted were:

726007/44/54/149/213
726223/322/338/429/438/448/489/499/531/579/633
726646/699/751/910/983/987

Photograph D. P. Rowland

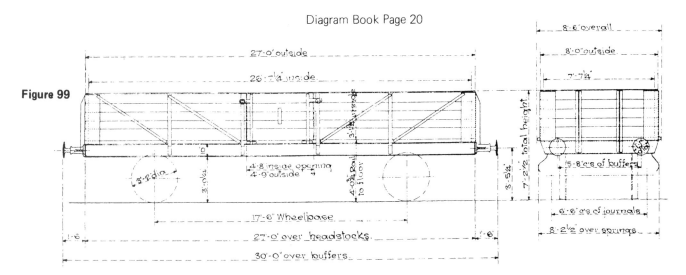

Figure 99

D1675 TUBE WAGON, LONG

Drawing No. 12/230 & 12/230A   **Figure 99**

Built to lot numbers 143–145/673/758/837/938/965

A total of 950 vehicles was built between 1925 and 1936 to this diagram, using two drawings. The 'A' amendment applied to final 600 built between 1933 and 1936, and the other drawing applied to the first 350 wagons constructed. The first 450 wagons were allocated random running numbers but the final 500 were numbered 499000–499299 and 499400–499599. Recorded random numbers by the author include: 6228, 10941, 13269, 300472, 339657, 341874. Almost certainly all the construction was in the grey livery with the large 'LMS' and these vehicles when repainted in bauxite would have been liveried in a manner similar to that employed with D1945. See **Plate 242**.

D1675
Code: TUW
Tare: 9 tons 5 cwt
Carrying capacity: 20 tons
'Morton' brake
Door on each side

Scale 0 1 2 3 4 5 6 7 8 9 10 feet

Plate 237 This picture shows an early example, No. 6228, that has not yet been branded 'Tube' or 'N'. It is possible that the early vehicles ran in traffic for some time before being marked in this way.

Photograph British Rail

Plate 238 A line of new construction with April 1936 paint dates at Charles Roberts with No. 499289 nearest the camera, beyond which can be seen Nos. 499292, 499291 and 499290. The 'A' drawing amendment is clearly visible as the earlier construction did not have the 'merchandise door' of the later vehicles.

*Photograph Charles Roberts
courtesy, National Railway Museum*

Plate 239 Wagon No. M499107, lettered both '20T' and '22T', was photographed in 1964 in grey and unpainted livery with 'Empty to Corby & Weldon' branding.

Photograph Author's Collection

20 TON LONG TUBE WAGON

Drawing No. 6638

No page number or figure

Only one vehicle existed for lot 314 and was officially recorded as both an ex-Government Disposal Board vehicle and as being built at Derby. This vehicle is illustrated in **Plate 240** and it will be noted that the general style is very similar to D1675, page 20, vehicles.

Plate 240

Photograph British Rail

D1945 TUBE WAGON (LONG)

Diagram Book Page 20A

Drawing Nos. 13/2292B
13/2292E
13/3419

Figure 100

Built to lot numbers 939/1032/1142/1320

In the same year that the final production of D1675 vehicles was being completed by Charles Roberts, Hurst Nelson had begun the construction of the first 100 tube wagons which were generally similar in outline but 3'6" longer overall. Between 1936 and 1942, a total of 900 wagons were constructed and they were numbered 499300–499399 and 499600–499999 and 492000–492399. Of these, probably only the first 100 carried the grey livery as depicted in **Plate 238**, the remainder being liveried as wagon No. 492183 depicted in **Plate 242**. No pictures exist to show the final 100 when first built and it is possible that they came out in 'unpainted livery'. Finally, it should be noted that, while D1675 were equipped with Morton brakes, the vehicles allocated to D1945 carried 20T standard brakes.

Figure 100

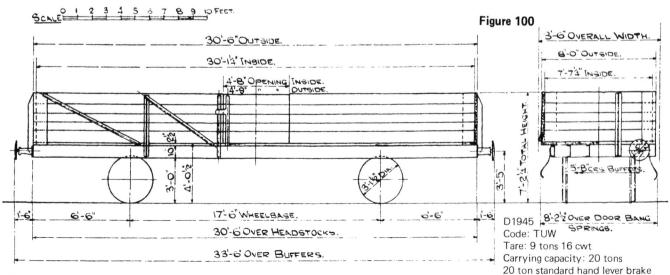

D1945
Code: TUW
Tare: 9 tons 16 cwt
Carrying capacity: 20 tons
20 ton standard hand lever brake

Plate 241

Plate 241 This illustrates wagon No. 499300 when first built in 1936. Photographed after delivery from Hurst Nelson.

Photograph British Rail

Plate 242

Plate 242 Wagon No. 492183 of lot 1142, built in 1939, displays the bauxite colour and livery style used for tube wagons.

Photograph British Rail

Plate 243 This illustrates wagon No. M499861 as running in 1964. Note the replacement axleboxes.

Photograph Author's Collection

Plate 243

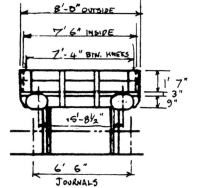

Figure 101

D1987A LONG TUBE WAGON

Diagram Book Page 20B

Drawing number not known

Figure 101

This interesting conversion took place in 1937 and the vehicle was numbered 28495 — probably being painted bauxite but no pictures are known to exist of the wagon.

D1987A
Code: TUW
Tare: 15 tons 18 cwt
Carrying capacity: 30 tons
Screw brake

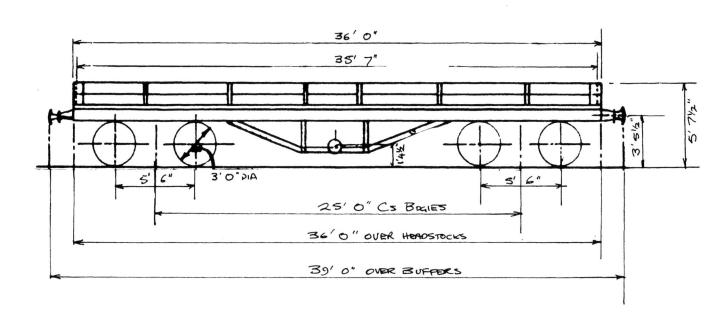

D2116 22 TON LONG TUBE WAGON

Drawing No. 13/3809

Figure 102

The 300 vehicles built to lot 1454 were constructed at Derby in 1947 and carried the running numbers 492400–492699 and, although to the same basic design as D1945, these wagons had corrugated steel ends, which were lined with wood.

Diagram Book Page 20C

D2116
Code: Tube
Tare: 10 tons 9 cwt
Carrying capacity: 22 tons
20 ton standard hand lever brake

SCALE: FEET.

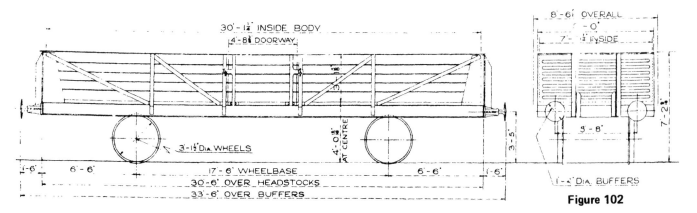

Figure 102

Plate 244

Plate 245

D1676 VENTILATED VAN

Diagram Book Page 21

Classified by BR as Goods Vans

Drawing No. 5669   **Figure 103**
Lots 36/251/2/3/
          5669B
Lots 337/8/342/369/370/387

These vehicles were very similar to D1664, page 9, but unlike that diagram, D1676 vehicles were ventilated. As noted on the diagram, the vans were built with hand brakes, through pipes and fully fitted and no doubt many of the non-fitted vans were equipped with vacuum brakes during their period of British Railways ownership.

A total of 2,956 vans were built between 1924 and 1928 and they were all allocated random numbers and the author has recorded the following: 7813, 98857, 20009, 159144, 186194, 186995, 191154, 204565, 212681, 212702, 230943, 305207.

A study of BR period pictures shows that a number of vans were fitted with tie rods between the axleboxes. Finally, it should be noted that the lot book originally allocated all these vehicles to page 9 which is D1664.

D1676
Codes,   hand brake only: V
             hand brake and through pipe: V
             fully fitted: FV
Tares,   hand brake only: 7 tons 6 cwt
             1 qr
             hand brake and through pipe:
             7 tons 7 cwt 3 qrs
             fully fitted: 7 tons 14 cwt 1 qr
Carrying capacity: 12 tons
'Morton' brake
Sliding door on each side
Dimensions marked thus * for wagons
fully fitted and with through pipes

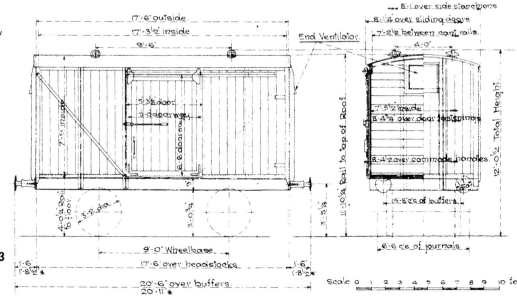

Figure 103

Plate 246 This picture of van No. 98857 is th̄
only known photograph of a vehicle in this seri¬
in LMS livery, having been taken in 1935.
Photograph British Ra

Plate 247 A 1960 picture of M186194 that
is rather interesting. The lot book records
that the 334 vans built in 1929 to lot 444
were produced to drawing No. 5645 and
allocated to D1832, but Derby Records
Office states that M186194 was built to
lot 444. The author is not sure where the
error lies and this volume allocates lot 444
to D1832 and M186194 to D1676.
Photograph D. P. Rowland

Plate 248 This picture of M212681 shows
a van from lot 253 as running in early BR
days. Note the strip welded across the vee
hanger; this practice was quite common
in the BR period.
Photograph Author's Collection

D1677 VENTILATED VAN

Classified by BR as Goods Vans

Drawing No. 5669/5814   **Figure 104**

A total of 50 vans only was built to lot 83 in 1925 and were allocated to this diagram.

No pictures exist and no running numbers are known. It will be seen from the diagram that these vehicles had twin vents at each end, an unusual practice for the LMS.

Figure 104

Scale 0 1 2 3 4 5 6 7 8 9 10 feet.

D1677
Codes,   hand brake only: V
         hand brake and through pipe: V
         fully fitted: FV
Tares,   hand brake only: 7 tons 4 cwt
         hand brake and through pipe: 7 tons 6 cwt
         fully fitted: 7 tons 10 cwt

Carrying capacity: 12 tons
'Morton' brake
Sliding door on each side
Some vans fitted with the two ventilators in each end only
Dimensions marked thus * for vans fully fitted and with through pipes

---

D1680 LONG LOW WAGON

Diagram Book Page 25

Drawing No. 14/1150   **Figure 105**

The lot book records a total of 187 vehicles built at Derby in 1927 to lot 327, but the original drawing number of 1584 was crossed out and 14/1150 was written down. Two running numbers only are known, namely 153930, 292523, and **Plate 249** is the only known illustration, showing No. 292523 at Derby. The lettering at the left hand end reads, 'N Tare 7.13.2 Load 20 Tons evenly distributed'.

Photograph British Rail

D1680
Code: LLW
Tare: 7 tons 13 cwt 2 qr
Carrying capacity: 20 tons
Double brake

Scale 0 1 2 3 4 5 6 7 8 9 10 feet.

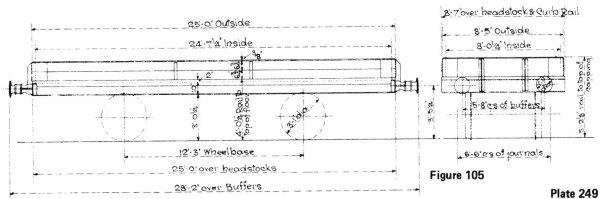

Figure 105

Plate 249

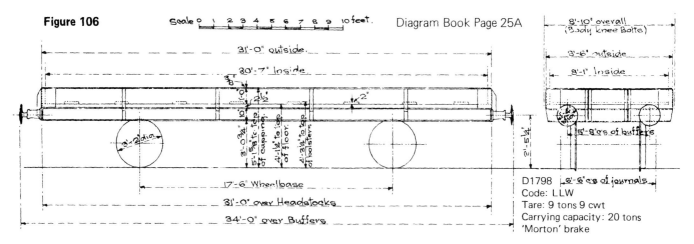

Figure 106

Scale 0 1 2 3 4 5 6 7 8 9 10 feet.

Diagram Book Page 25A

8'-10" overall
(Body knee Bolts)

3'-6" outside

8'-1" Inside

31'-0" outside.

30'-7" Inside

5'-8' c's of buffers

D1798
Code: LLW
Tare: 9 tons 9 cwt
Carrying capacity: 20 tons
'Morton' brake

6'-6" c's of journals

17'-6" Wheelbase

31'-0" over Headstocks

34'-0" over Buffers

3'-2" dia.

D1798 LONG LOW WAGON

Drawing No.   **Figure 106**

Built to lot numbers 455/533

A total of 400 long low wagons were built in 1930 and allocated to this diagram. Block numbers were not used and the author has only been able to record 43160, 43330, 43720, 45461, 46346, 46480, 324599, 352649. These vehicles were built with fixed sides and equipped with Morton brakes. When first constructed, they would have carried grey livery as illustrated in **Plate 250** but, in due course, when repainted in bauxite, their appearance would have resembled wagon No. 497736 in **Plate 256**.

Plate 250 This 1939 view of wagon No. 45461 displays the livery when built. Note that there is an 'N' at each end but no 'Long Low' branding on the body, which was normally on the solebar below the running number.

Photograph A. E. West

Plate 251

Plate 250

Plate 251 This picture of wagon No. 324599 shows an alternative method of livery style employed when first built.

Photograph British Rail

Plate 252

Plate 252 Photographed in 1939 wagon No. 43160 is now in bauxite livery and is branded 'Long Low'.

Photograph A. E. West

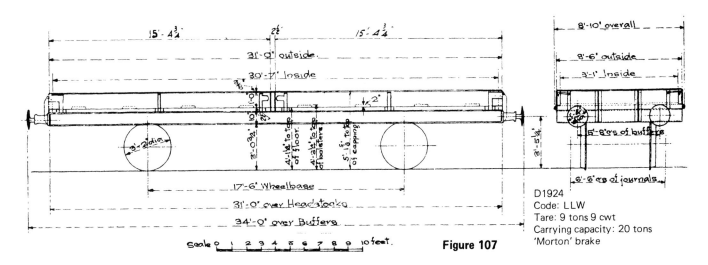

D1924
Code: LLW
Tare: 9 tons 9 cwt
Carrying capacity: 20 tons
'Morton' brake

Figure 107

D1924 20 TON LONG LOW WAGON

Diagram Book Page 25B

Drawing No. 13/2060 lot 836 & 1215
13/2060B lot 926
13/2060D lot 968
13/2060F lot 1005
13/2060G lot 1143

Lot numbers as above

Figure 107

All these vehicles were built at Wolverton and the reason for the various amended drawings is not entirely known. Totalling 1,325 wagons, built between 1933 and 1940, they carried running numbers 497000–498324. The early construction, possibly up to 497735, came out in grey with large 'LMS', then from at least 497736, **Plate 256**, it was still in grey but with the small 'LMS'. However, from about 497775, bauxite was almost certainly the body colour employed.

Plate 253

Plate 253 A Wolverton view of No. 497006, showing an example of the first 250 wagons built at Wolverton and the strapping on the sides and iron work on the solebar immediately below the vertical strapping on this early construction should be compared with the wagon illustrated in **Plate 254**.

Photograph British Rail

Plate 254 This illustrates wagon No. 497359, built in 1936, and here the modification to the side strapping can be seen.

Photograph A. E. West

Plate 254

Plate 255

Plate 255 An unidentified vehicle, photographed in 1964, which clearly illustrates the interior construction of these vehicles.

Photograph Author's Collection

Plate 257

Plate 256 No. 497736 displays the insignia change from large to small size letters on a grey body.

Photograph British Rail

Plate 257 This final picture confirms the British Railways uprating of capacity to 22 tons and change of designation from long low to plate wagon; M498098 was built in 1939 and is seen as running in 1964.

Photograph Author's Collection

D2069 20 TON LONG LOW WAGON

Diagram Book Page 25C   Drawing 13/3414   **Figure 108**

D2069
Code: LLW
Tare: 9 tons 10 cwt
Carrying capacity: 20 tons
20 ton standard hand lever brake

The 300 vehicles allocated to this diagram were all built at Wolverton in 1942 to lot 1321 and numbered 498325—498624 and, unlike the previous construction, were 4'0" less in length. Almost certainly they were ex-works in the 'unpainted livery' of that period.

27'-0" OUTSIDE
26'-7" INSIDE
13'-4¾" DOOR   13'-4¾" DOOR
4'-2⅝"   3'-0⅜"   5'-1" TO TOP OF DOORS   3'-1½" DIA   3'-5"
17'-6" WHEELBASE
27'-0" OVER HEADSTOCKS
30'-0" OVER BUFFERS
1'-6"   1'-6"

8'-11⅝" OVER HINGES
8'-1" INSIDE
1'-1" DIA
5'-8" CENTRES BUFFERS
8'-6" OVER HEADSTOCKS & SIDE DOORS

Figure 108

SCALE 0 1 2 3 4 5 6 7 8 9 10 FEET

Plate 258

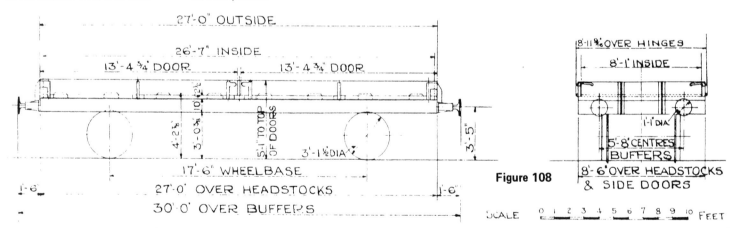

Plate 258 This 1966 view illustrates No. M498535 in BR ownership, condemned at Hunslet.

Photograph Author's Collection

D2083 LONG LOW WAGON   Diagram Book Page 25D

Drawing No. 12/651   **Figure 109**

Built to lot numbers 1344/1355/1367/1385/1514

The final long lows, by now designated plate wagons, were built between 1944 and 1949 and carried running numbers 498625–498874 and 496000–496249. Of these, 496200–249 came out in BR ownership and never carried any LMS livery.

D2083
Code: LLW
Tare: 9 tons 6 cwt
Carrying capacity: 22 tons
20 ton standard hand lever brake

Figure 109

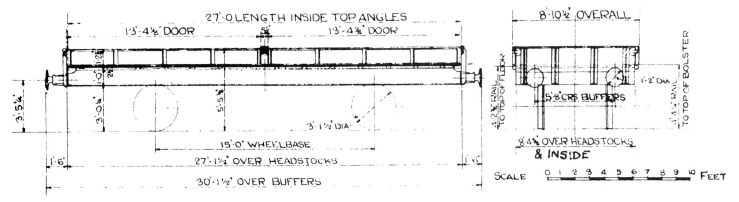

Plate 259 This illustrates wagon No. 498866 as built in March 1944. The vehicle is painted bauxite and is designated 'Plate'.
Photograph British Rail

Plate 260 No. M496230 in BR livery should be compared with No. 498866, **Plate 259**, with particular reference to the lack of rivets along the bottom of the side.
Photograph British Rail

Plate 260

Plate 261

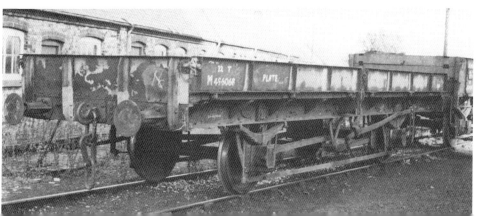

Plate 261 This 1964 picture shows M496068 in British Railways ownership. Note the instanter coupling and tie rod between the axleboxes.
Photograph Author's Collection

Plate 262

Diagram Book Page 26

D1681 DEAL WAGON

Drawing Nos. 1618 lot 351
          14/1158 lot 404
          14/1158 lot 710
          14/2742 lot 1023

Built to lot numbers 351/404/710/1023

Figure 110

Plate 262 This illustrates wagon No. 86123 in ex-works condition and the location of the 'LMS' on the solebar is interesting. Note the double side brakes which were a feature of these wagons.

Photograph British Rail

A total of 250 deal wagons was built by the LMS and only the final 50 built in 1937 were allocated block numbers 490000–490049, the others built in 1928 and 1933 carried random numbers of which only 86123 and 326379 have been recorded. It is interesting to note that each of the four lots built had a different drawing number.

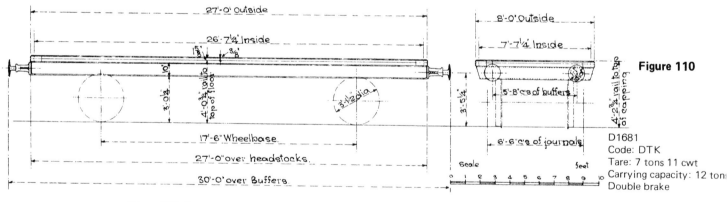

Figure 110

D1681
Code: DTK
Tare: 7 tons 11 cwt
Carrying capacity: 12 ton
Double brake

Plate 263 This illustrates No. 490007 of the final lot built in 1937 and shows a grey colour wagon with the post-1936 style of small 'LMS'. No doubt bauxite repaints would have been similarly lettered.

Plate 263

Photograph British Rail

D1689 GRAIN VAN

Drawing No. 11/176 lots 373/402/723/755/833 **Figure 111**

           11/176A lot 924

           11/176B lot 1019

           Lot 1208 drawing No. is not clear in the lot list

A total of 105 vehicles were built between 1928 and 1940 and the lots up to and including 755 carried random numbers of which 168875, 299022, 299030 have been recorded. Starting with lot 833 block numbers commenced and they ran from 701300—701354. Of these numbers, 701345—701354 were never in grey and entered service in bauxite livery similar to No. 701351 depicted in **Plate 266**. It is possible that Nos. 701310—701344 entered service in grey livery but with post-1936 small size 'LMS' normally associated with the bauxite livery.

Attention is drawn to the question of the drawing numbers and in particular to the roof profile of No. 701351. Lot 2009 built by British Railways also had this more rounded roof profile which started with lot 1208, Nos. 701345—701354.

D1689
Code: BGV
Tare: 10 tons 1 cwt
Carrying capacity: 20 tons
Cubic capacity: 1,200 cu. ft.
Independent brake at each end of van
1 side trap door, 1 bottom outlet, 2 sliding doors in roof

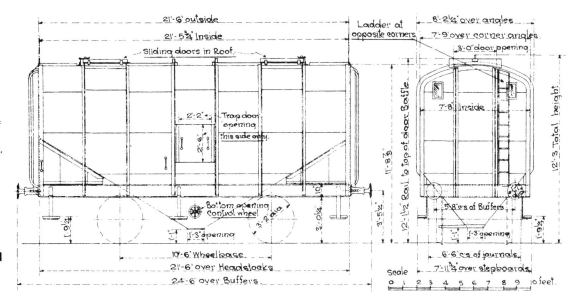

Figure 111

Plate 264

Plate 264 This illustrates No. 168875 of lot 373 built in 1928. A picture of No. 299022 is identical except that 20T and 'Tare 9.19.3' is visible and possibly this vehicle had not been weighed at the time of the photograph which is dated 31st October, 1928.

Photograph British Rail

Plate 265 No. 701314 is an example of lot 924 and carries a November 1936 paint date. The grey body of this vehicle incorporates an insignia normally associated with vehicles painted in bauxite. A picture of No. 701320, built by Charles Roberts, also shows a grey painted vehicle with the small size insignia except that it is lettered 'LMS 20 TONS 701320' in the panel where 'LMS 701314' appears on **Plate 265** and 'BULK GRAIN', in the same panel, is painted in letters of the same size. These subtle variations all tend to make it very difficult to record livery detail variations.

Photograph British Rail

Plate 266 A 1940 view of No. 701351, clearly illustrating the post-1936 bauxite livery and the rounded roof ends of the final construction.

Photograph British Rail

D1817 BEER VAN

Drawing No. 13/1160 **Figure 112**

100 vehicles to carry beer were built at Derby in 1929 to lot 419 and, surprisingly for this period, carried block numbers 189331—189430. The Midland never had any beer vans and, to the best of the author's knowledge, only the LNWR within the LMS group allocated vehicles to this traffic, so it is suggested that this batch replaced life-expired LNWR vehicles. No other pictures of these vans exist and it is not entirely possible to say how they were liveried in the post-1936 period. One imagines they followed contemporary covered goods van practice but the author cannot be certain. Almost certainly, they ran in blocks and it is unlikely that they would have been seen singly.

Finally, it should be noted that the official drawing shows extra cross braces on the ends but the diagram and the only photograph does not show their existence.

Figure 112

D1817
Code: BRV
Tare: 7 tons 4 cwt 3 qrs
Carrying capacity: 12 tons
Hand brake
Sliding door on each side
Lot 419

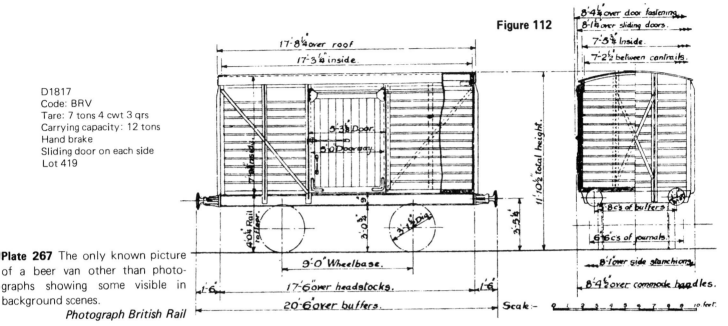

Plate 267 The only known picture of a beer van other than photographs showing some visible in background scenes.

Photograph British Rail

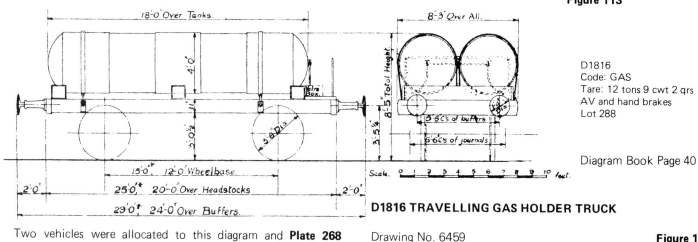

Figure 113

D1816
Code: GAS
Tare: 12 tons 9 cwt 2 qrs
AV and hand brakes
Lot 288

Diagram Book Page 40

D1816 TRAVELLING GAS HOLDER TRUCK

Drawing No. 6459

Figure 11[...]

Two vehicles were allocated to this diagram and **Plate 268** illustrates truck No. 278472. It will be noted that the vehicle has an ex-LNWR chassis and appears to be carrying passenger style livery. However, it is not possible to say what the body colour was — crimson lake, black or slate grey but it was probably crimson in this instance.

Photograph Author's Collection

Built to lot number 288

The section comprising pages 40—45A covers the variou[...] designs of vehicles used to carry gas for supplying kitchen car[...] which used this fuel for cooking. The quantities built were ver[...] small and often second hand underframes were employed.

Plate 268

D1815 TRAVELLING GAS HOLDER TRUCK

Drawing No. 6428

Figure 114

Built to lot numbers 311/416/514/563

10 trucks were allocated to this diagram and three lot numbers appear on the diagram. However, the lot book also allocates lot 311 to this diagram.

No pictures are known to exist and no running numbers have been recorded.

Diagram Book Page 41

D1815
Code: GAS
Tare: 13 tons 6 cwt 2 qrs
AV and hand brakes
Lots 416, 514, 563

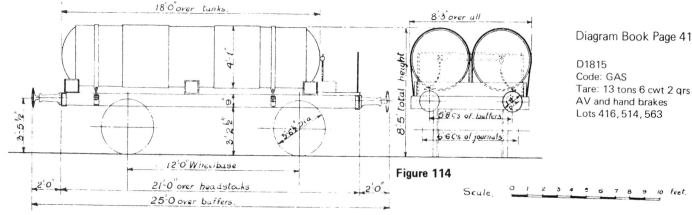

Figure 114

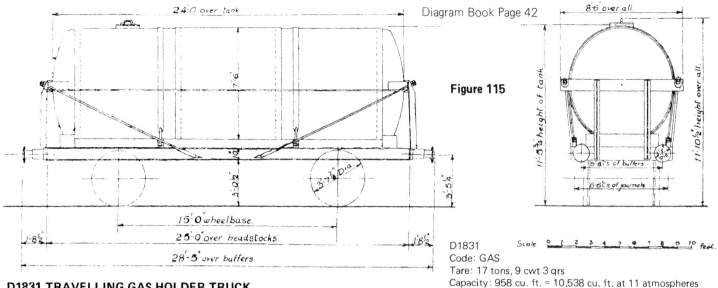

Diagram Book Page 42

Figure 115

D1831
Code: GAS
Tare: 17 tons, 9 cwt 3 qrs
Capacity: 958 cu. ft. = 10,538 cu. ft. at 11 atmospheres
AV and hand brakes
Lot 359

D1831 TRAVELLING GAS HOLDER TRUCK

Drawing No. 14/1099   **Figure 115**

Built to lot number 359

Three trucks were built by Charles Roberts in 1928 and two
numbers have been recorded, namely Nos. 31916 and 31897:
both vehicles are illustrated in **Plate 269.**

Plate 269 This illustrates Nos. 31897 and 31916 in original
condition prior to delivery from the makers. This clearly
shows vehicles in grey livery but whether they were repainted
in bauxite after 1936 is not known.

Photograph Charles Roberts, courtesy National Railway Museum

D1827 TRAVELLING GAS HOLDER TRUCK

Drawing No. 13/1475   **Figure 116**   Diagram Book Page 43

One vehicle only, built in 1930 at Derby to lot 568, was
constructed on a second hand underframe. No pictures are
known to exist and the running number is not known.

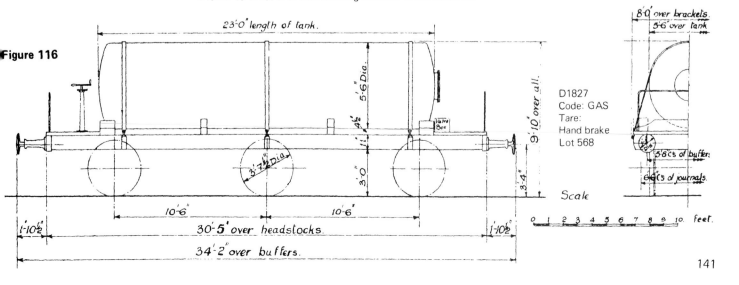

Figure 116

D1827
Code: GAS
Tare:
Hand brake
Lot 568

D1826 TRAVELLING GAS HOLDER TRUCK   Diagram Book Page 44

Drawing No. 13/1476   **Figure 117**

Built to lot number 567
This diagram covered the four vehicles built at Derby in 1930 and no
pictures are known to exist, although the author has recorded two running
numbers: 217279 and 317229.

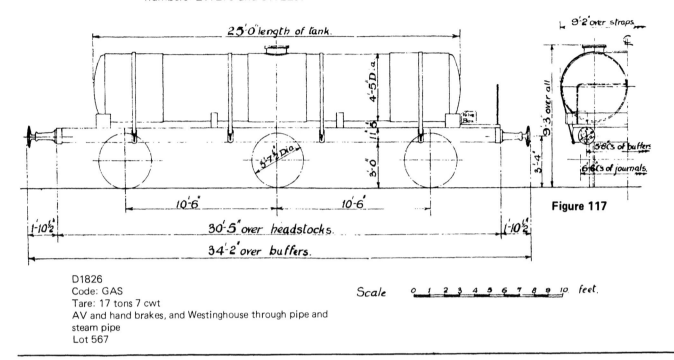

Figure 117

D1826
Code: GAS
Tare: 17 tons 7 cwt
AV and hand brakes, and Westinghouse through pipe and
steam pipe
Lot 567

Scale 0 1 2 3 4 5 6 7 8 9 10 feet.

D1825 TRAVELLING GAS HOLDER TRUCK   Diagram Book Page 45

Drawing No. 14/1711   **Figure 118**

Built to lot number 566
Two vehicles were built at Derby in 1930 and the running numbers are
not known. It will be noted that secondhand LNWR underframes were
used but it is not clear what livery was employed.

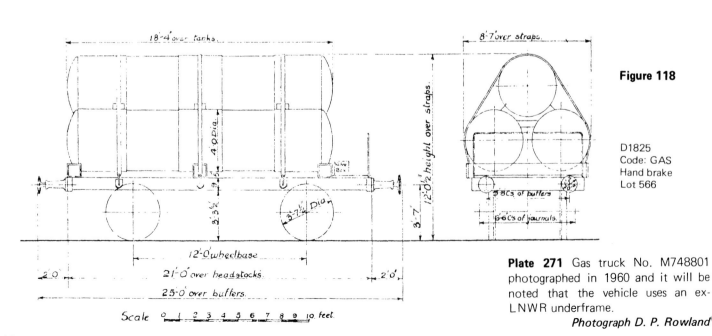

Figure 118

D1825
Code: GAS
Hand brake
Lot 566

Plate 271 Gas truck No. M748801
photographed in 1960 and it will be
noted that the vehicle uses an ex-
LNWR underframe.
Photograph D. P. Rowland

Plate 270

Plate 270 illustrates a gas holder truck, believed to be an example of D1825.

Photograph Author's Collection

Diagram Book Page 45A

Figure 119

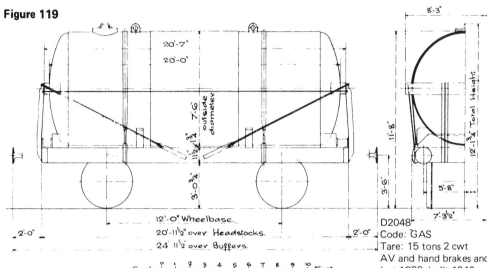

20'-7"
20'-0"

7'-6" outside diameter

11½"
3'-0¾"

12'-0" Wheelbase.
20'-11½" over Headstocks.
24'-11½" over Buffers.

2'-0"   2'-0"

Scale 0 1 2 3 4 5 6 7 8 9 10 Feet

8'-3"

11'-8"

12'-13¾" Total Height.

3'-6"

5'-8"

7'-3½"

D2048
Code: GAS
Tare: 15 tons 2 cwt
AV and hand brakes and steam pipe
Lot 1233, built 1940

D2048 TRAVELLING GAS HOLDER TRUCK

Drawing No. 13/3168   **Figure 119**
3192

Four trucks numbered 748800–748803 were built to lot 1233 at Derby in 1940 and they may have entered traffic in bauxite livery and, while this is probable, it is by no means certain. No official photograph appears to have been taken, but fortunately a picture of one of these vehicles in British Railways ownership exists (**Plate 271**).

Plate 271

Figure 120

Plate 272

Scale. 0 1 2 3 4 5 6 7 8 9 10 feet.

Diagram Book Page 46

D1820
Code: GAS
Tare: 8 tons 9 cwt
Carrying capacity: 10 tons
Net capacity: 2,066 gallons
Double brake
Lot 475

D1820 CREOSOTE TANK WAGON

Drawing No. 13/2676A   **Figure 120**

Built to lot numbers 475/1160
Ten vehicles were built by Charles Roberts
— 9 in 1929 and 1 in 1938 — and three
running numbers have been recorded: Nos.
189979 and 304592 from the 1928 batch
and No. 748900 built in 1938.

Plate 272 illustrates tank No. 304592 when
constructed in 1929. The post-1936 livery
is not known.

Plate 273 This ex-works picture of No.
748900, taken in the Charles Roberts' yard,
clearly shows the solitary example of lot
1160 built in 1938 and it should be
compared, both in livery and construction,
with No. 304592 of lot 475, illustrated in
Plate 272 and built to the same diagram.

Photographs Charles Roberts,
courtesy, National Railway Museum

Plate 273

D2031
Tare: 9 tons 3 cwt 2 qrs
Carrying capacity: 14 tons
Net capacity: 3,062 gallons
'Morton' brake
Steam heating

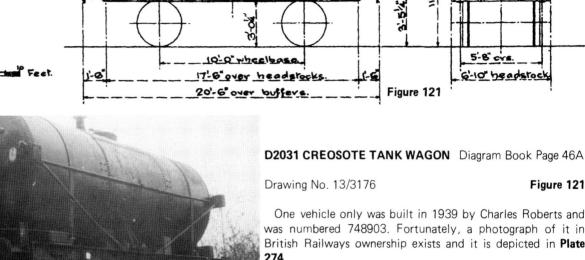

Figure 121

Scale

Plate 274

D2031 CREOSOTE TANK WAGON   Diagram Book Page 46A

Drawing No. 13/3176   **Figure 121**

One vehicle only was built in 1939 by Charles Roberts and was numbered 748903. Fortunately, a photograph of it in British Railways ownership exists and it is depicted in **Plate 274**.

Photograph D. Larkin

Plate 275

D2033 CREOSOTE TANK WAGON   Diagram Book Page 46B

Drawing No. 13/2676   **Figure 122**

Two vehicles were built by Charles Roberts in 1939 and it is interesting to compare pages 46A and 46B which formed lots 1235 and 1236, and it is difficult to understand why two different designs were produced for the same traffic.

Plate 275 Built in 1939 as the only example of lot 1236 No. 748903 does not appear to be in bauxite livery but seems to be in grey. Note that the LMS and running number is smaller than on 748900 in **Plate 273**.

Photograph Charles Roberts, courtesy National Railway Museum

D2033
Code: GAS
Tare: 8 tons 11 cwt
Carrying capacity: 10 tons
Net capacity: 2,066 gallons
'Morton' brake
Lot 1235

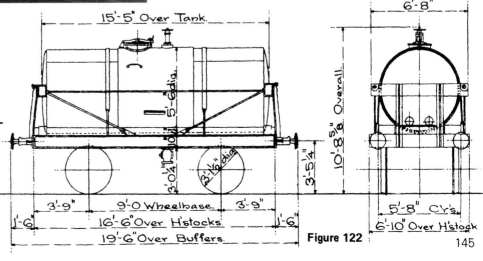

SCALE.   FEET.

Figure 122

D2060 AMMONIACAL LIQUOR TANK

Drawing No. Not known   **Figure 123**
Lot Number Not known

Very little is known about this vehicle — no pictures, to

the author's knowledge, exist but fortunately the running number 198608 appears on the diagram.

One can only presume that it was painted grey but what form the lettering took and if there was any special branding, one can only speculate.

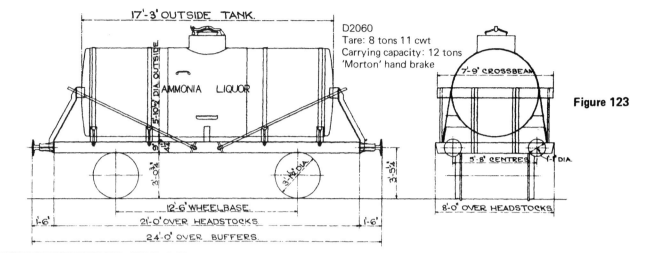

    Figure 124

D1823 CONTAINER TRUCK

Drawing No. 13/1327   **Figure 124**

1,000 wagons were recorded as being converted at Derby in 1930/1 to lot 518 and it is difficult to see what alterations were made to the original vehicles which were, in effect, ex-Midland Railway wagons to D305.

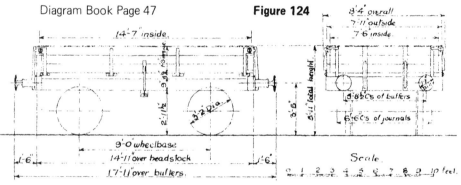

D1823
Code: MG
Tare: 4 tons 16 cwt
Double brake
Both sides hinged
Converted from 8 ton low-sided wagons
Lot 518

Plate 276 This illustrates a 'B' type container loaded into an open wagon No. 13259. However, the paint date on the wagon records 10th January, 1929, and so this was not a converted wagon and the brakes were on one side only. In the container section, *Volume Two*, examples of open goods wagons, in container traffic will be noted.

Photograph British Rail

D2062 CHASSIS FOR 'BR' CONTAINER

Figure 125

These vehicles were built using milk tank underframes, probably in 1937. No further details are known.

D2062
Code: CC
Tare: 6 tons 15 cwt
AV and hand brakes and steam pipe
Converted from milk tank underframes

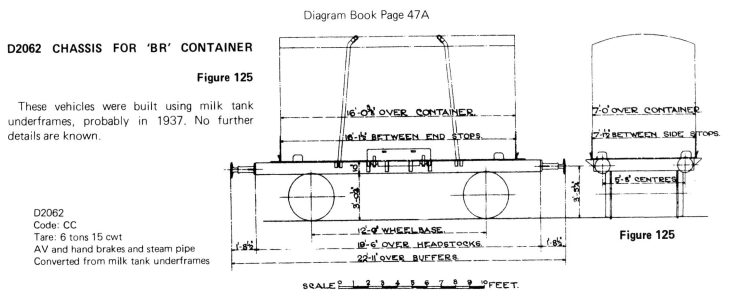

Figure 125

D2063 CHASSIS FOR 'BM' CONTAINER

Figure 126

Converted from milk tank underframes, probably in 1937. No further details are known.

D2063
Code: CC
Tare: 6 tons 5 cwt
AV and hand brakes and steam pipe
Converted from milk tank underframes

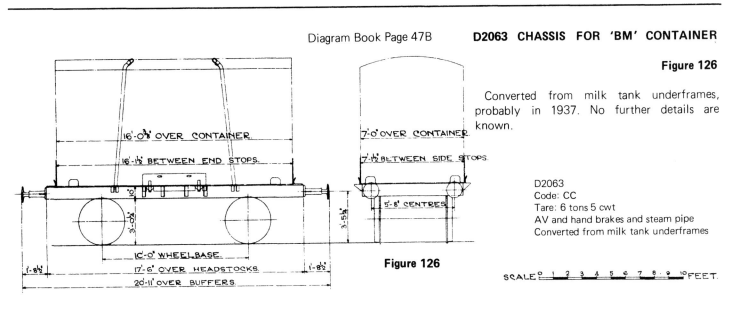

Figure 126

D2064 CHASSIS FOR 'BM' CONTAINER

Figure 127

Converted from milk tank underframes, probably in 1937. No further details are known.

D2064
Code: CC
Tare: 6 tons 7 cwt
AV and hand brakes and steam pipe
Converted from milk tank underframes

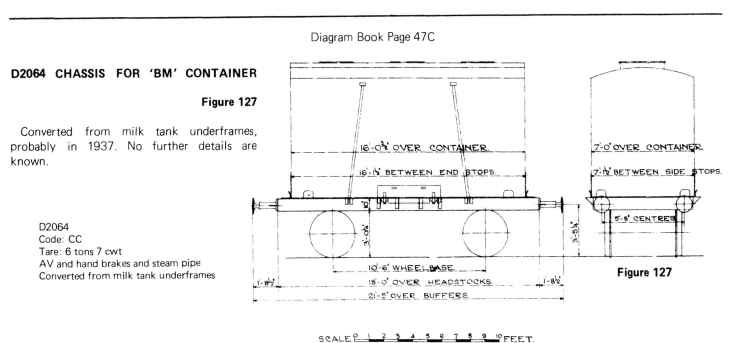

Figure 127

147

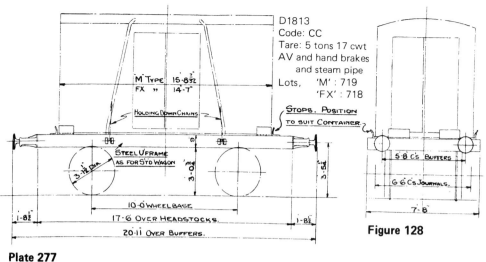

Plate 277

D1813 CHASSIS FOR 'M' AND 'FX' CONTAINERS   Diagram Book Page 48

Drawing No. 13/1915   **Figure 128**

Built to lot numbers 718/719

260 chassis were built at Wolverton for 'M' and 'FX' containers in 1933/4 and only three numbers have been recorded: 231982, 232196 and 237061.

Plate 277 This illustrates chassis No. 231982 when constructed and a further picture appears in the container chapter, *Volume Two,* showing truck No. 232196 with an 'FR' container.

Photograph British Rail

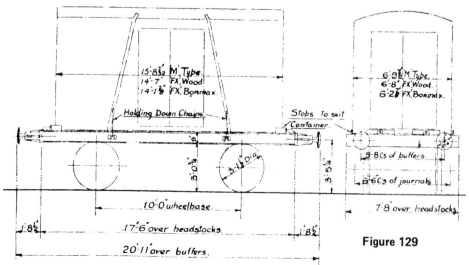

Figure 129

D1838 CHASSIS FOR 'M' AND 'FX' CONTAINERS   Diagram Book Page 49

Drawing No. 13/1738B   **Figure 129**

Built to lot numbers 667/679

40 chassis were built at Derby in 1932/3 and three running numbers have been recorded: Nos. 199970/84/87, and it is possible that this was part of a batch of consecutive numbers.

D1838
Code: CC
Tare: 5 tons 19 cwt 2 qrs
Fully fitted and steam pipe
Lots, 667, 679

Plate 278 This illustrates chassis No. 199970 with an 'M' type container. Two other D1838 chassis are illustrated in the container section in *Volume Two*.

Photograph British Rail

Plate 279 This picture shows chassis No. 705084 of lot 890 with a 'BR' container. A further picture of a D1975 chassis appears in the container section, *Volume Two*.

Photograph British Rail

D1975 CHASSIS FOR 'BR' CONTAINER

Drawing No. 13/2159B lot 890
13/2347 lot 972
13/2159 lot 1216

Figure 130

115 vehicles were produced during the period 1935—1939 and were numbered 705070—705169 and 705570—705589 and this final batch entered traffic in bauxite livery. It is interesting to note that three different drawings were used and it is not known what detail alterations were made.

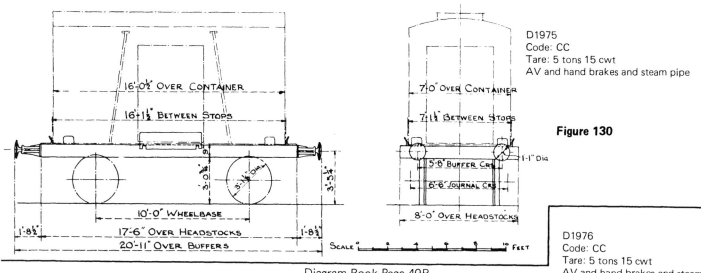

D1975
Code: CC
Tare: 5 tons 15 cwt
AV and hand brakes and steam pipe

Figure 130

16'-0½" OVER CONTAINER
16'-1½" BETWEEN STOPS
3'-0½"
3'-1½" Dia.
3'-5¼"
10'-0" WHEELBASE
17'-6" OVER HEADSTOCKS
20'-11" OVER BUFFERS
1'-8½"
1'-8½"

7'-0" OVER CONTAINER
7'-1½" BETWEEN STOPS
1-1" Dia
5'-8" BUFFER CRS
6'-6" JOURNAL CRS
8'-0" OVER HEADSTOCKS
SCALE 0 FEET

D1976
Code: CC
Tare: 5 tons 15 cwt
AV and hand brakes and steam pip

D1976 CHASSIS FOR 'FM' CONTAINER

Drawing No. 13/2197 lot 888/889
13/2348 lot 973/4/5
13/2348A lot 1057/8

Figure 131

470 chassis were built between 1935—37 and were numbered 705000—705069, 705170—705569. While most entered traffic in grey livery, it is possible that some of the 1937 construction, Nos. 705370—705569, left the works in bauxite.

Scale 0 feet

Plate 280 This picture illustrates chassis No. 705453 in original condition.

Photograph British Rail

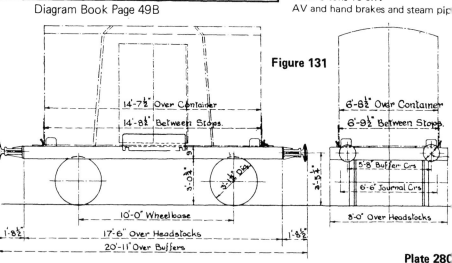

Figure 131

14'-7½" Over Container
14'-8½" Between Stops
3'-0½"
3'-1½" Dia
3'-5¼"
10'-0" Wheelbase
17'-6" Over Headstocks
20'-11" Over Buffers
1'-8½"
1'-8½"

6'-8½" Over Container
6'-9½" Between Stops
5'-8" Buffer Crs
6'-6" Journal Crs
8'-0" Over Headstocks

Plate 280

Plate 281

Plates 281, 282, 283 and **284** These four pictures illustrate chassis No. 705379 as running in 1939 and these pictures have been included to assist model makers.

Photograph A. E. West

Plate 282

Plate 284

Plate 283

D2065 CHASSIS FOR 'FM' AND 'FR' CONTAINERS Diagram Book Page 49C

Drawing No. 13/3311   **Figure 132**

100 chassis numbered 705590—705689 were built at Derby to lot 1301 in 1941 and were turned out in bauxite livery.

Regrettably, no official pictures appear to have been taken to illustrate these vehicles.

D2065
Code: CC
Tare: 5 tons 15 cwt
AV and hand brakes and steam pipe

SCALE 0 1 2 3 4 5 6 7 8 9 10 FEET.

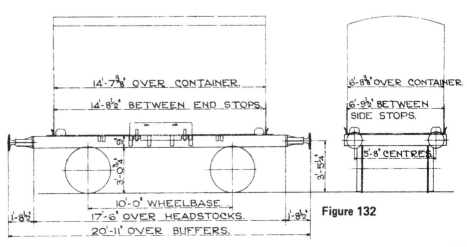

14'-7⅜" OVER CONTAINER.

14'-8½" BETWEEN END STOPS.

6'-8⅜" OVER CONTAINER.

6'-9½" BETWEEN SIDE STOPS.

5'-8" CENTRES.

3'-0¾"

3'-5¼"

10'-0" WHEELBASE.

17'-6" OVER HEADSTOCKS.

20'-11" OVER BUFFERS.

1'-8½"   1'-8½"

Figure 132

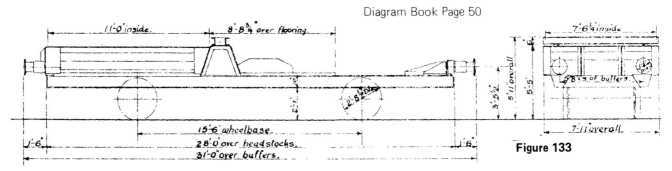

Figure 133

D1836 MATCH WAGON FOR 36 TON BREAKDOWN CRANE

Drawing No. 11/230   **Figure 133**

A total of 6 vehicles numbered 299850–299855 were built to lot 600 at Derby in 1931, and **Plate 285** illustrates No. 299852 when first built in what appears to be a dark grey livery.

Photograph British Rail

Scale

D1836
Code: none allocated
Tare: 9 tons 3 cwt
Weight of wedges, tools etc. not to exceed 2 tons
Hand brake and through vacuum pipe
Lot 600

Plate 285

Plate 286 This picture, taken in 1970, illustrates DM299851 at Crewe and clearly shows how a match wagon ran in service.

Photograph Author's Collection

Plate 286

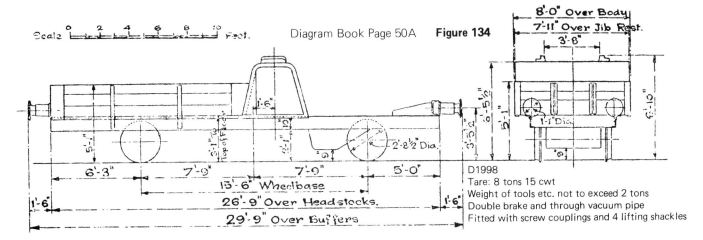

Scale [0 2 4 6 8 10] Feet.

8'-0" Over Body
7'-11" Over Jib Rest.
3'-8"

D1998
Tare: 8 tons 15 cwt
Weight of tools etc. not to exceed 2 tons
Double brake and through vacuum pipe
Fitted with screw couplings and 4 lifting shackles

6'-3" — 7'-9" — 7'-9" — 5'-0"
13'-6" Wheelbase
26'-9" Over Headstocks.
29'-9" Over Buffers
1'-6"
2'-8½" Dia.

Plate 287 shows the vehicle when first built in what appears to be a dark grey livery. Although the author is not able to be certain of the exact body colour, there is some suggestion that the colour adopted may have matched the crane; in which case, it may have been either black or red.

Photograph British Rail

D1998 MATCH WAGON FOR 36 TON BREAKDOWN CRANE

Drawing No. 13/2571   **Figure 134**

One vehicle only was built at Derby in 1937 to lot 1069 and it carried the running number 770000.

Plate 287

Plate 288 This c1939 picture illustrates the vehicle in service and the additional wooden box should be noted.

Photograph A. E. West

Plate 288

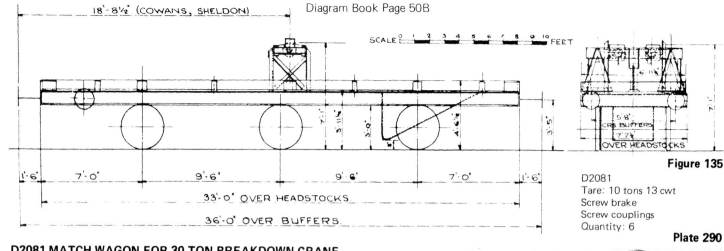

SCALE 0 1 2 3 4 5 6 7 8 9 10 FEET

18'-8½' (COWANS, SHELDON)

7'-1"
3'-11½"
3'-0"
4'-6½"
3'-5"

1'-6' 7'-0' 9'-6' 9'-6' 7'-0' 1'-6'

33'-0' OVER HEADSTOCKS

36'-0' OVER BUFFERS.

Figure 135

D2081
Tare: 10 tons 13 cwt
Screw brake
Screw couplings
Quantity: 6

Plate 290

D2081 MATCH WAGON FOR 30 TON BREAKDOWN CRANE

Drawing No. 13/3450   **Figure 135**
        13/3450B

Built to part lot 1324 & lot 1336

A total of six vehicles were built at Wolverton in 1942 and were numbered 770006—770011.

Two official photographs were taken and they are illustrated in **Plates 289** and **290**. These pictures seem to show a black body and light grey solebar on wagon No. 770011.

Photographs British Rail

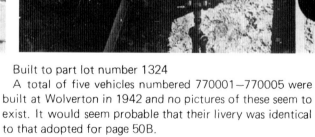

D2082 MATCH WAGON FOR 30 TON BREAKDOWN CRANE

Drawing No. 13/3450   **Figure 136**

Built to part lot number 1324

A total of five vehicles numbered 770001—770005 were built at Wolverton in 1942 and no pictures of these seem to exist. It would seem probable that their livery was identical to that adopted for page 50B.

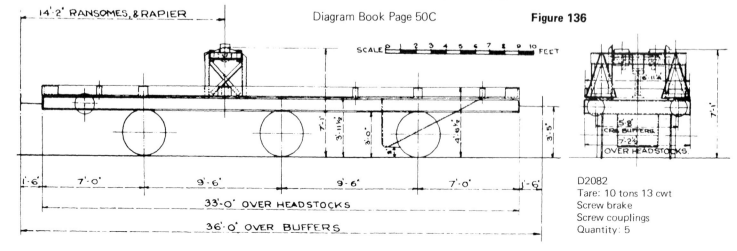

Figure 136

14'-2' RANSOMES, & RAPIER

SCALE 0 1 2 3 4 5 6 7 8 9 10 FEET

7'-1"
3'-11½"
3'-0"
4'-6½"
3'-5"

1'-6' 7'-0' 9'-6' 9'-6' 7'-0' 1'-6'

33'-0' OVER HEADSTOCKS

36'-0' OVER BUFFERS

D2082
Tare: 10 tons 13 cwt
Screw brake
Screw couplings
Quantity: 5

D1888 SAND WAGON

Drawing No. 13/2079   **Figure 137**

These 100 vehicles built at Derby in 1934 and numbered 403900–403999 were to carry sand for the construction industry.

D1888
Code:
Tare: 6 tons 19 cwt
Carrying capacity: 12 tons
Cubic capacity: 408 cu. ft.
'Morton' hand brake
Lot 842

Plate 291

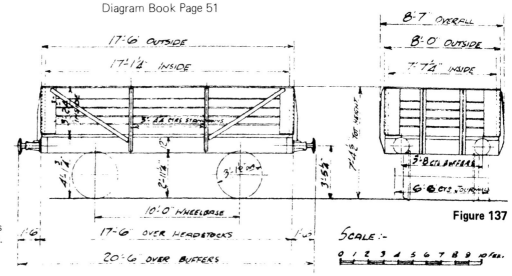

Figure 137

Plate 291 This picture illustrates wagon No. 403921 in its original condition and it will be seen that it is, in effect, an open merchandise wagon but without side doors. Special attention was paid to their construction to ensure that the planks did not have any gaps between them to allow the sand to escape.

Photograph British Rail

Plate 292 This illustrates M403993 as running in 'unpainted' BR livery with black patches onto which the numbers, branding, etc was painted, including 'Sand, Empty to Leighton Buzzard LMR'.

Photograph D. S. Field

Plate 292

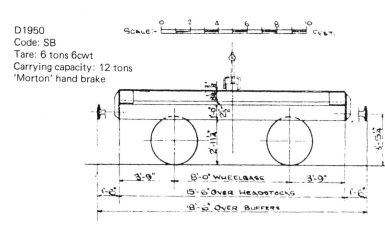

D1950
Code: SB
Tare: 6 tons 6cwt
Carrying capacity: 12 tons
'Morton' hand brake

SCALE:- 0 2 4 6 8 10 FEET.

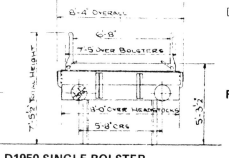

Figure 138

D1950 SINGLE BOLSTER

Drawing No. 13/2393A

Figure 13

Plate 293 This illustrates No. 722101 of lot 977 with a '4.5.36' paint date and it is interesting to note the 'N' non common user markings which do not appear on other vehicles.

Built to lot numbers 977/1105/1201

Numbered 72200–723249, these 1,250 wagons were built a Derby between 1936 and 1939 and, when first constructed carried three different liveries.

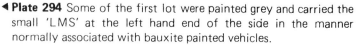

◄**Plate 294** Some of the first lot were painted grey and carried the small 'LMS' at the left hand end of the side in the manner normally associated with bauxite painted vehicles.

Photographs British Rail

Plate 295 This picture of wagon No. 722722 clearly shows the ▶ bauxite livery when new and, as mentioned, some of the later examples of lot 977 carried this style of lettering but still with a grey body colour.

Photograph British Rail

Plate 295

D2041 SINGLE BOLSTER

Drawing 13/3278 **Figure 139**

The 162 vehicles built to lot 1280 at Derby in 1940 and numbered 723250–723411 differed from the previous construction in the use of steel, not wooden solebars. Regrettably, no photographs appear to exist showing these vehicles.

Diagram Book Page 52A

D2041
Code: SB
Tare: 5 tons 19 cwt
Carrying capacity: 12 tons
'Morton' hand brake

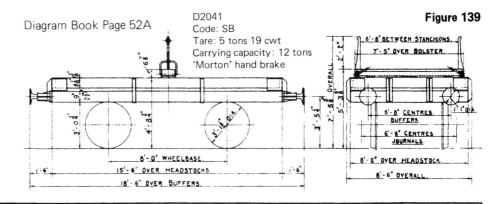

Figure 139

D1951 20 TON SODA ASH WAGON   Diagram Book Page 53

Drawing No. 14/2691 **Figure 140**

The author is not clear what type of vehicle was originally used for soda ash traffic prior to the introduction of these 'special traffic wagons' in 1936. 10 wagons were built at Derby to lot 971, numbered 689000–9.

Figure 140

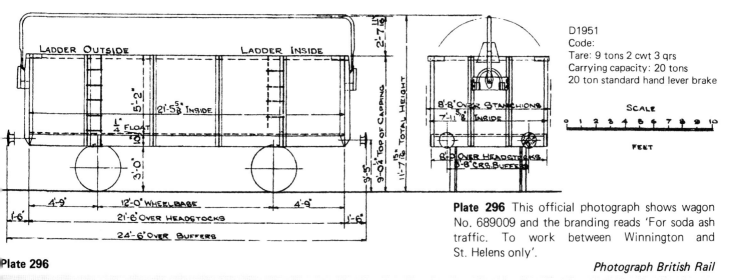

D1951
Code:
Tare: 9 tons 2 cwt 3 qrs
Carrying capacity: 20 tons
20 ton standard hand lever brake

Plate 296 This official photograph shows wagon No. 689009 and the branding reads 'For soda ash traffic. To work between Winnington and St. Helens only'.

Photograph British Rail

Plate 296

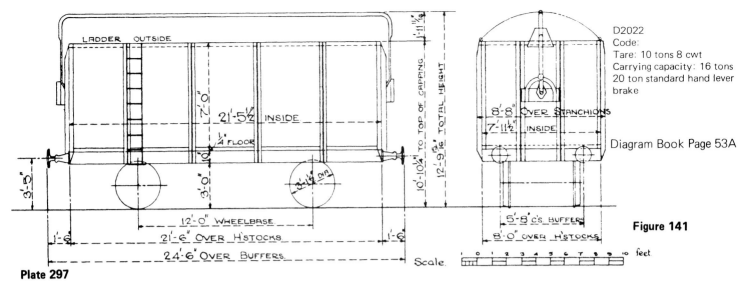

D2022
Code:
Tare: 10 tons 8 cwt
Carrying capacity: 16 tons
20 ton standard hand lever brake

Diagram Book Page 53A

Figure 141

Plate 297

D2022 16 TON SODA ASH WAGON

Drawing No. 14/2689   **Figure 141**
14/3143

50 wagons numbered 689100–689149 were built at Derby in 1939 to lot 1155 and it is interesting to note that, compared with page 53, these wagons had a larger body but a lower rated carrying capacity. It should also be noted that they never ran in grey livery during LMS ownership.

Plate 297 This picture illustrates wagon No. 689143 in original condition and the branding reads 'Fleetwood to Silvertown'.
Photograph British Rail

Plate 298 This has been included to show the interior of these wagons and, in particular, the arrangement of the ladder. It is not clear if these vehicles had ladders on both sides.

Photograph British Rail

Plate 299 This 1965 picture shows No. M689106 in service and the branding reads 'Return Empty to Pendleton (Brindle Heath)'. Note that the tarpaulin rail has been removed.

Photograph Author's Collection

D2128 20 TON SODA ASH WAGON Diagram Book Page 53B

Drawing No. 12/753A   **Figure 142**

It is interesting to note that the lot book records that lot 1469 comprised 6 LNER vehicles and 15 LMS wagons, and so the author presumes that the running numbers were 689300-20. The paint date on the solebar reads '9.8.48' so these wagons were never anything other than British Railways vehicles.

Plate 300 The example illustrated here, No. M689300, shows that, whereas earlier vehicles had open tops, these were built as hopper wagons with covered tops.

Photograph British Rail

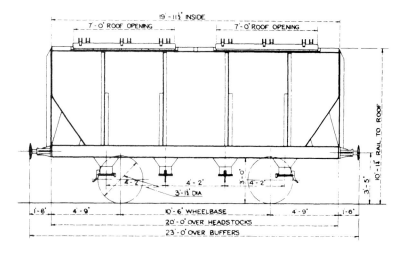

D2128   **Figure 142**
Code:
Tare: 10 tons 17 cwt
Carrying capacity: 20 tons
'Morton' brake

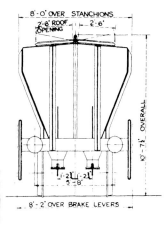

Plate 300

D1953 SLEEPER WAGON

Diagram Book Page 54

Drawing No. 14/2738
The last two lots 14/3572

Figure 143

Built to lot numbers 979/1078/1163/1217/1270/1284.
It would seem that enough pre-grouping vehicles were available for this traffic during the early LMS period and it was not until 1936 that the construction of new wagons commenced. During the period 1936–1939, 259 wagons were built carrying running numbers 749000–749258. Examination of various pictures of service vehicles suggests that both red oxide and grey livery was employed and reference to the photograph captions will reveal what is known, in greater detail.

Figure 143

D1953
Tare: 6 tons 6 cwt
Carrying capacity: 12 tons
'Morton' brake

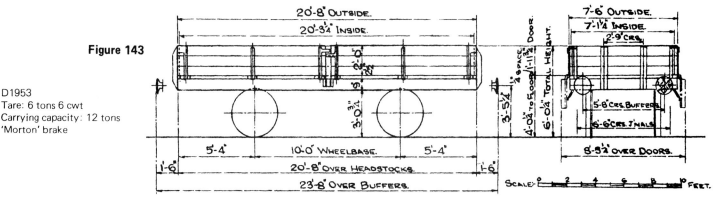

Plate 301 This illustrates wagon No. 749002 in original condition and the wagon appears to be in red oxide livery.

Photograph British Rail

Plate 302 A 1964 picture illustrating a wagon (DM749071) in British Railways ownership that appears to be in grey body colour.

Photograph Author's Collection

Plate 302

D2098 SLEEPER WAGON

Diagram Book Page 54A

Drawing No. 14/4030

Figure 144

Built to lot numbers 1365/1427/1480

The wartime use of thinner planks resulted in a new diagram being issued in 1944 to cover the 200 vehicles built between 1944 and 1947 carrying running numbers 749259–749458. It is believed that all these wagons entered traffic in the 'unpainted' livery, depicted in **Plate 303**.

D2098
Tare: 6 tons 6 cwt
Carrying capacity: 12 tons
'Morton' brake

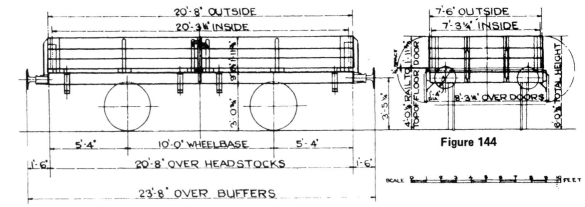

Figure 144

Plate 303

Plate 303 This illustrates wagon No. 749426 of lot 1480 built in 1947, prior to entering traffic, and it is a very clear example of how wooden bodied wagons were finished during this period.

Photograph British Rail

D1954 BALLAST WAGON

Drawing No. 14/2737 lots 978–1218
Lots 1285/1318, 14/3591 only

Figure 145

Built to lot numbers 978/1029/1106/1107/1209/1218/1285/1318

It would appear that the need to replace life expired ballast wagons occurred in 1936 and caused the arrival of this new standard design. A number of lots were produced to the original drawing and then a new drawing was issued for the final 1941/2 construction. During the period 1936/1942, 2,760 wagons were built, carrying running numbers 740000–742759 and, like the sleeper wagons, there is some doubt about the livery employed and reference to what is known appears in the captions.

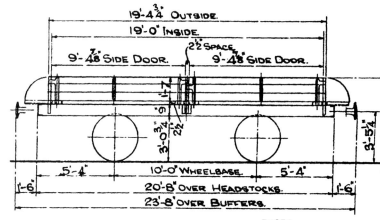

D1954
Tare: 6 tons 8 cwt
Carrying capacity: 12 tons
'Morton' brake

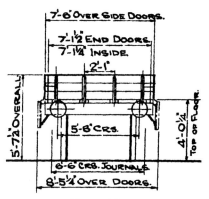

Figure 145

Plate 304

Plate 304 Wagon No. 740059 built in 1936, appears to be in grey livery.

Photograph British Rail

Plate 305 No. 740008 was part of lot 978 which included No. 740059, **Plate 304**. The paint dates are '26.5.36' for No.740008 and '15.6.36' for No. 740059 and it can be seen that a change of colour from red oxide to grey occurred.

Photograph British Rail

Plate 305

Plate 306

Plate 306 Wagon No. 740432 was built in 1937, and is seen as running in 1939. It would seem that this vehicle is in grey body colour.

Photograph A. E. West

Plate 307 Wagon No. 740726, built in 1938, has a dark body colour, almost certainly red oxide. Note the branding which is a little different from normal.

Photograph British Rail

D2095 BALLAST WAGON   Diagram Book Page 55A

Drawing No. 14/3880   **Figure 146**

Built to lot numbers 1347/1389/1426/1479

Between 1944–47 a further 400 ballast wagons were constructed and, apart from the thickness of the plank sides, they were identical in construction to D1954, page 55. They were numbered 742760–743159 and their livery was similar to the final examples constructed to D1954.

Plate 308 This picture has been selected to show a wagon in Briti Railways ownership. No. DM741032 was built in 1938 and the vie shows the inside of the vehicle, including the inside strapping.

Photograph D. Lark

Plate 310 Wagon No. 742813 in ex-works conditio It is worth comparing with No. 742948 (**Plate 309**) see the subtle differences with the paintwork whic then carried the livery details.

Photograph British Ra

Plate 311 This picture of No. DM743135 taken 1968 shows the 'unpainted' livery style of the perio

Photograph A. E. We

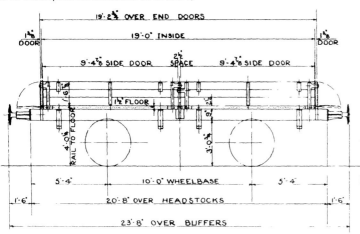

D2095
Tare: 6 tons 10 cwt
Carrying capacity: 12 ton
'Morton' brake

Figure 146

Plate 309 This illustrates No. 742948 in ex-works condition
Photograph British Ra

Plate 310

Plate 311   D1973 20 TON LOCO COAL WAGON   Diagram Book Page 56

Drawing No. 14/2740D   **Figure 147**

Built to lot numbers 990—992

In 1936/7 the LMS built a quantity of steel bodied locomotive coal wagons via the trade and used two diagrams for what were visually identical vehicles — the difference between these diagrams being only the type of steel employed and this is noted on the diagrams.

The copper bearing steel vehicles totalled 500 wagons, numbered 750000—750499 and it would seem that the original construction entered traffic with a grey body colour and with the small size 'LMS', normally associated with the later bauxite — see **Plate 315** which shows an example of D1974 built in October 1936. Regrettably, only one picture of these wagons in pre-1948 livery exists but reference to D1974 will reveal what was happening in livery and detail variations.

Plate 312 This illustrates No. 750114 following the fitting of the extra steelwork in the corners and over the angle iron on the sides. It is not known exactly when these modifications took place. Note the patch and new tare weight. Body colour is grey but the insignia is in the style normally associated with the bauxite body colour.

Plate 313 This illustrates M750361 in BR livery, as running after the end of steam locomotives and, as seen, depicts the later style of BR lettering.

Photograph D. Larkin

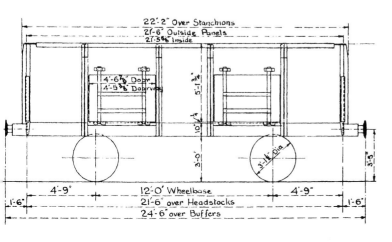

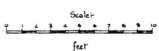

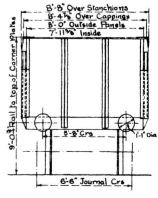

Figure 147

Figure 148

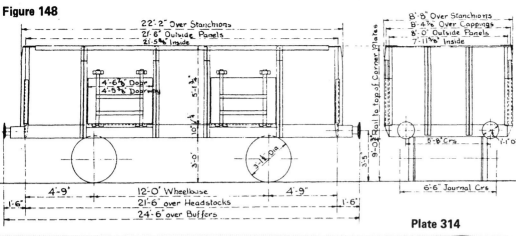

22'-2" Over Stanchions
21'-6" Outside Panels
21'-5⅜" Inside

4'-6⅝" Door
4'-5⅝" Doorway

5'-1¼"

10'¾"

3'-0"

3'-1⅛" Dia.

4'-9"   12'-0" Wheelbase   4'-9"
21'-6" over Headstocks
24'-6" over Buffers
1'-6"   1'-6"

8'-8" Over Stanchions
8'-4⅜" Over Cappings
8'-0" Outside Panels
7'-11⅝" Inside

Rail to top of Corner Plates

9'-0"

3'-5"

5'-8" Crs
1'-1" Dia.
6'-6" Journal Crs

Diagram Book Page 56A

D1974
Code: LW
Tare: 10 tons 3 cwt
Carrying capacity : 20 tons
20 ton standard hand lever brake

Scale:
0 1 2 3 4 5 6 7 8 9 10 feet

D1974 20 TON LOCO COAL WAGON

Drawing No. 14/2740D **Figure 148**
Lots 993/4
Lot 1366/1388 — 12/681
Lot 1425 — 12/681/B

This diagram dealt with wrought iron wagons and, while 500 copper bearing wagons were produced, 500 wrought iron vehicles entered traffic in 1936/7 numbered 750500—750999, lots 993/4, 751000—751349 lots 1366/1388 1425 and it will be seen that the same drawing number was used for this first 1,000 wagons but, in 1945, a new drawing was issued and this may have had something to do with the modifications which will be noted in **Plate 312** when compared with **Plate 314**. The corners and side angles were protected by extra ironwork and these modifications took place at an early date as seen in **Plate 312** which shows a D1973 vehicle.

Plate 314 No. 750602 is a very early example of a wagon built in October 1936 and should be compared with another early example illustrated in **Plate 312**.
Photograph British Rail

Plate 315 In 1946 No. 751167 was constructed and this picture illustrates the wagon in bauxite livery and the modifications to the body will be noted.
Photograph British Rail

Plate 314

Plate 315

Plate 316

Plate 316 Photographed in 1962, this shows No. M751095 in revenue service although still branded 'LOCO'.
Photograph D. P. Rowland

D2038
Code: LW
Tare: 6 tons 14 cwt
Carrying capacity: 13 tons
'Morton' brake
Lot 1207

Figure 149

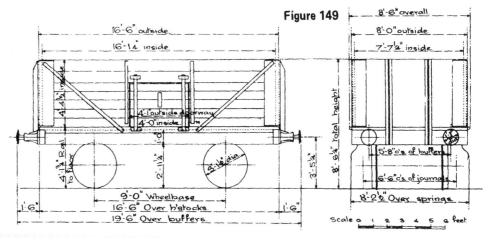

Plate 317 This illustration of No. M757162 is the only picture known to exist and depicts the vehicle at the end of its active life.

Photograph D. Larkin

D2038 13 TON LOCO COAL WAGON

Drawing No. 13/3181   **Figure 149**

Running numbers 757000–757253
Built Derby 1940 lots 1207/1265
For some reason a total of 254 13 ton wooden bodied vehicles was produced and it is difficult to know why they were built when construction of 20 ton vehicles had already commenced. The diagram shows wooden solebars and head-stocks but the ends of the diagram are not shown planked. However, reference to **Plate 317** reveals that these vehicles did not have steel ends and this is the only picture known to exist. They entered traffic carrying bauxite livery and would have been similar to D1671, **Plate 198**.

Plate 317

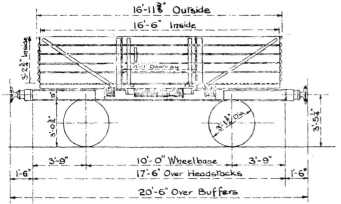

Figure 150

D1979   **Plate 318**
Code: SAW
Tare: 7 tons 6 cwt 2 qrs
Carrying capacity: 12 tons
'Morton' brake

D1979 SHOCK ABSORBING WAGON   Diagram Book Page 57

Drawing No. 13/2436 U/f   **Figure 150**
14/2820 Body

One prototype only, numbered 450000 was built to this diagram and it is illustrated in **Plate 318**.

Plate 318 This depicts No. 450000 when first produced in 1937 and when built it did not have lined ends although no doubt it was later altered to conform with D1983 and received the white stripes.

Photograph British Rail

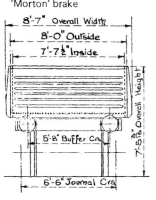

D1983 SHOCK ABSORBING WAGON

Drawing No. 13/2436 U/F **Figure 151**
14/2820 Body

Built to part lot 1060/lots 1231/1266/ 1465

After building the prototype in 1937 a further 699 were built between 1938 and 1949 and were numbered 450001–450499 and 450500–450749. Of these, up to 450449 were built by 1940 and these probably entered traffic in bauxite livery, while 450500–450749 were unpainted — See **Plate 320**.

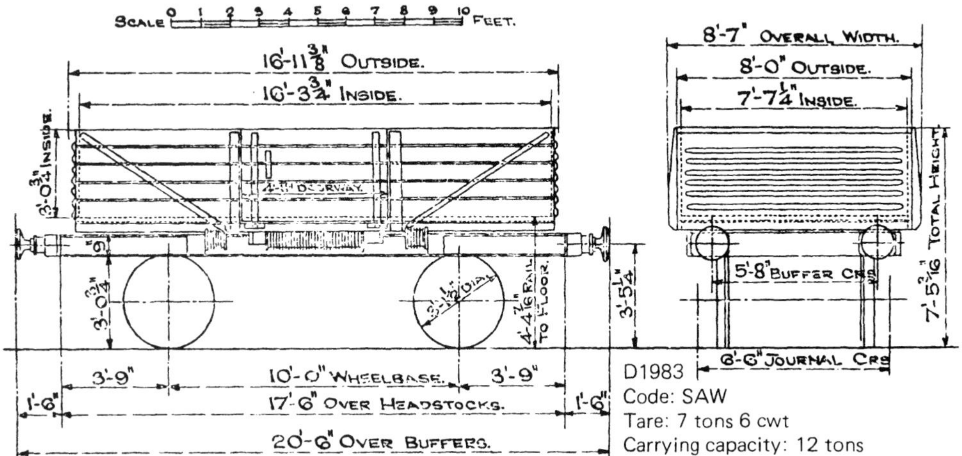

SCALE 0 1 2 3 4 5 6 7 8 9 10 FEET.

16'-11⅜" OUTSIDE.
16'-3¾" INSIDE.
3'-0½" INSIDE.
4-8" DOORWAY.
9"
3'-0¼"
4-4 16" RAIL TO FLOOR.
3'-5¼"
3'-9" 10'-0" WHEELBASE. 3'-9"
1'-6" 17'-6" OVER HEADSTOCKS. 1'-6"
20'-6" OVER BUFFERS.

8'-7" OVERALL WIDTH.
8'-0" OUTSIDE.
7'-7¼" INSIDE.
7'-5 16" TOTAL HEIGHT.
5'-8" BUFFER CRS.
6'-6" JOURNAL CRS

D1983
Code: SAW
Tare: 7 tons 6 cwt
Carrying capacity: 12 tons
'Morton' brake

Figure 151

Plate 319 This illustrates No. 450007 in bauxite livery, seen in service shortly after construction.

Photograph British Rail

Plate 319

Plate 320 This picture taken in 1949 shows an LMS wagon built by British Railways and carrying the unpainted livery of this period. Note the edging to the white stripes on the unpainted wood.

Photograph British Rail

Plate 321 Photographed in 1964, M450529 has been equipped with automatic vacuum brakes. It was originally a 'hand brake only' vehicle. It has a tie bar between the 'W' irons and is fitted with replacement open spoke wheels.

Photograph Author's Collection

Plate 322 This illustrates No. 450497 in service and is seen being loaded with glass at Pilkingtons Glass Works.

Photograph Pilkington Bros. Ltd.

Plate 322

D2040 SHOCK ABSORBING WAGON

Diagram Book Page 57B

Drawing No. 14/3062 Body
13/3803 U/F

Figure 152

Built to lot numbers 1267/1466

A total of 94 wagons, generally similar to D1983 but fitted with automatic vacuum brakes was built in 1940 (50) and 1949 (44), numbered 450450—450499, 450750—450793. The 1940 vehicles entered traffic in bauxite while the 1949 wagons were unpainted and carried the 'M' prefix of British Railways. It should be noted, however, that many examples of D1983 were later modified to D2040 — see Plate 321.

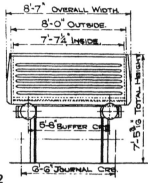

D2040
Code: SAW
Tare: 8 tons 15 cwt
Carrying capacity: 12 tons
Fully fitted and 'Morton' hand brake
Lot 1267
Built 1940

Figure 152

Plate 323

Plate 324

Plate 323 Photographed in 1952, No. M450498 is an example of a 1940 wagon in early BR days. By now, white stripes are visible on the end of the wagon and the wagon is branded 'Empty to Overseal LMR'.

Photograph A. E. West

Plate 324 This picture shows M450774 which entered traffic in 1949 as a British Railways vehicle in the 'unpainted' livery of the period. Note the spoked, not disc, wheels.

Photograph British Rail

D2152
Code: Shock
Tare: 8 tons 8 cwt without cradles
       9 tons 2 cwt with cradles
Carrying capacity: 13 tons
Fully fitted and 'Morton' hand brake

Figure 153

D2152 SHOCK ABSORBING WAGON

Drawing No. 14/4633A

Figure 153

A total of 6 medium type wagons were built at Derby in 1949 to lot 1546 numbered M489000—M489005 for glass traffic. They were fitted with automatic vacuum brakes but it is interesting to note the use of open spoke wheels. Regrettably, only one picture is known to exist and this is reproduced as **Plate 325**.

Plate 325 This illustrates No. M489004 with a '21.4.49' paint date. The wagon is painted in bauxite and does not employ the 'unpainted' style used with some vehicles at this time.

Photograph British Rail

D1986 12 TON ONE PLANK WAGON

Diagram Book Page 58

Drawing No. 13/2552

Figure 154

Built to lot numbers 1113/1114

One thousand wagons of this type were built by the LMS in 1938 and, as befits their date of introduction to traffic, never carried the grey body colour. The original construction was hand brake only but they were later uprated to 13 ton carrying capacity and many were equipped with automatic vacuum brakes by BR.

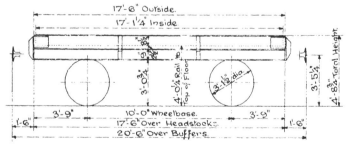

Figure 154 Scale.

D1986
Code: LG
Tare: 5 tons 6 cwt
Carrying capacity: 12 tons
'Morton' hand brake

Plate 326 No. 460030, as built in March 1938.

Photograph British Rail

Plate 327 This photograph, taken on 3rd September, 1938, illustrates No. 460621 loaded with furniture removal container No. K297, which itself was originally painted in crimson lake. The paint date visible on the solebar reads '22.7.38' so the wagon has only been in traffic for a few weeks.

Photograph A. E. West

D1988 UNDERFRAME FOR ROAD/RAIL EDIBLE OIL TANKS
Diagram Book Page 59

Drawing No. 13/2603   **Figure 155**

Built to lot number 1079

The lot book describes these as 'Tanks for Whale Oil' but the diagram suggests edible oil! Eight chassis were built at Derby in 1938 and carried the numbers 707000—707007. The livery was black solebars and below with bauxite above.

Plate 328 By 1964 M460741 has received new axleboxes, automatic vacuum brakes, a tie bar between the 'W' irons, one pair each of open and solid spoke wheels and new buffers.

Photograph Author's Collection

D1988
Code: TUF
Tare: 16 tons 10 cwt
Carrying capacity: 18 tons

AV and hand brakes and steam pipes
Electric immersion heaters in tanks
Fitted with accumulators and dynamo

SCALE |0 2 4 6 8 10| FEET.

Figure 155

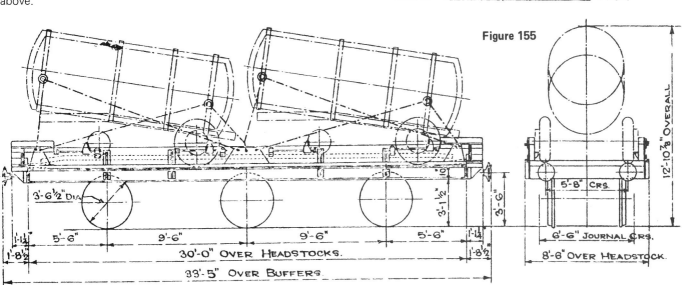

Plate 329 This illustrates No. 707005 in ex-works condition.

Photograph British Rail

Plate 330 This shows the method of loading two tanks onto a chassis by means of an end loading ramp.

Photograph British Rail

Plate 330

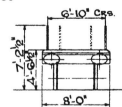

D1985
Tare: 23 tons 10 cwt
Carrying capacity: 50 tons
Compound lever brake

SCALE 0 1 2 3 4 5 6 7 8 9 10 FEET.

D1985 50 TON BOGIE RAIL TRUCK

Diagram Book Page 60

Figure 156

In certain respects this diagram is out of place within this section. These vehicles were transferred to the special wagon book, where full details will be found under the reference, page 19C — (see *Volume Two*).

Figure 156

48'-0" CRS. OF BOGIES.
62'-0" OVER HEADSTOCKS.
65'-0" OVER BUFFERS.

D2003 MATCH WAGON TO ARMOUR PLATE TRUCK   Diagram Book Page 61

Drawing number not known   **Figure 157**

Not very much is known about this diagram. It cannot be found in the lot book and no running numbers are recorded beyond the fact that a note on page 2A (see *Volume Two*) records that two vehicles for match purposes, Nos. 116347/8, were kept at Sheffield.

Figure 157

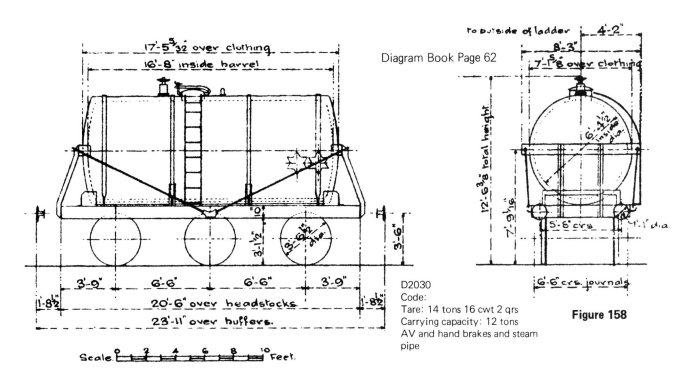

D2003
Tare: 13 tons 1 cwt
Double brake

Note: vehicles lettered 'Not to be Loaded. For use as Check Wagons Only'

Diagram Book Page 62

D2030
Code:
Tare: 14 tons 16 cwt 2 qrs
Carrying capacity: 12 tons
AV and hand brakes and steam pipe

Figure 158

D2030 TANK WAGON FOR CABLE COMPOUND

Drawing No. 14/3441 lot 1239   **Figure 158**
14/4443 lot 1492

Built to lot numbers 1239/1492

Two wagons were built for this traffic, one in 1939 and one in 1947, numbered 707300/1. No photographs are known to exist and therefore the livery details cannot be given. It is believed that they were designed to carry jointing compound — a black solid bituminous substance for use when high tension cables were joined together.

D2034 CHASSIS FOR LOCH KATRINE WATER TANK   Diagram Book Page 63

Drawing No. 13/3155   **Figure 159**

Built to lot 1237
A single vehicle was built at Derby in 1939 and is illustrated in **Plate 331**. It is interesting in that the tank was finished in GWR coach livery due to the presence of a Mr. Norris, a noted 7mm scale GWR modeller on the Board of Portal, Dingwall & Norris Ltd.

Figure 159

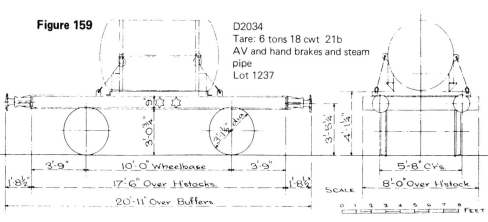

D2034
Tare: 6 tons 18 cwt 21b
AV and hand brakes and steam pipe
Lot 1237

Plate 331 illustrates No. 707200 in original condition. The LMS chassis would no doubt be all black in colour.

Photograph British Rail

D2135 CHASSIS FOR SODIUM SILICATE TANK

Drawing No. 14/4517   **Figure 160**

A single tank was built in 1947 to lot number 1539 but, regrettably, no pictures are known to exist and so it is not possible to record its livery or running number.

SCALE [scale bar] FEET

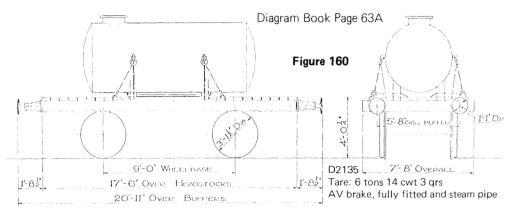

Diagram Book Page 63A

Figure 160

9'-0" WHEELBASE
17'-6" OVER HEADSTOCKS
20'-11" OVER BUFFERS
3'-1½" Dia
1'-8½"
1'-8½"

4'-0¼"
5'-8" CRS. BUFFERS
1'-1" Dia
D2135   7'-8" OVERALL
Tare: 6 tons 14 cwt 3 qrs
AV brake, fully fitted and steam pipe

Figure 161   SCALE [scale bar]

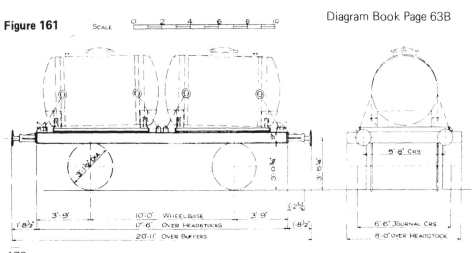

Diagram Book Page 63B

3'-1½" DIA
3'-0¾"
3'-5¼"
3'-9"
10'-0" WHEELBASE
3'-9"
17'-6" OVER HEADSTOCKS
20'-11" OVER BUFFERS
1'-8½"
1'-8½"
1'-2½"

5'-8" CRS
6'-6" JOURNAL CRS
8'-0" OVER HEADSTOCK

D2141 CHASSIS FOR DEMOUNTABLE LOCH KATRINE WATER TANKS

Drawing No. 13/3923   **Figure 161**

Built in 1949, British Railways chassis No. M707201 to lot 1490 was for use with two Lemon Hart & Son tanks. While the tank chassis was painted black it is not known for certain what colour the Lemon Hart tanks were painted. See **Plate 332** (facing page, top).

Photograph British Rail

D2141
'Morton' brake, fully fitted and steam pipes
Lot 1490

Plate 332

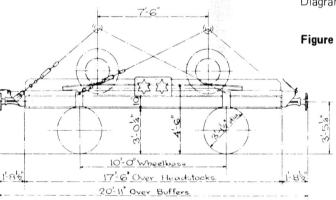

Diagram Book Page 64

Figure 162

D2035
Code: TUF
Tare: 9 tons 3 cwt
Carrying capacity: 10 tons
AV and hand brakes
Lot 1230

SCALE

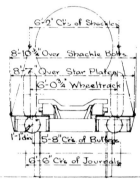

Plate 333

D2035 CHASSIS FOR ROAD/RAIL BEER TANKS

Drawing No. 12/547 lot 1230   **Figure 162**
    14/4164 lot 1419 U/frame
    13/3659 lot 1419 Body

Totalling 15 vehicles, numbered 707100—707104 (built in 1939) and 707108—707117, this series was probably painted all black, except for the edge of the floor which was bauxite.

Plate 333 This illustrates No. 707100 in original condition and should be compared with 707109 in **Plate 334**. Note the detail differences of wheels, livery and general construction.

Photographs British Rail

Plate 334

D2037 TANK WAGON FOR BEER

Drawing No. 14/3515

Diagram Book Page 65

Figure 163

Built to lot numbers 1241/1380/1437

Four tank wagons were constructed to three lots of two, one built in 1939, 1944 and 1947, numbered 707105/6 707107 and 707118 respectively. A photograph of the 1944 built vehicle is provided in **Plate 335**. The solebar and below was blac but it is not known for certain what was the colour of the tank o the lettering thereon. Nor is it known for which breweries th other tanks were branded.

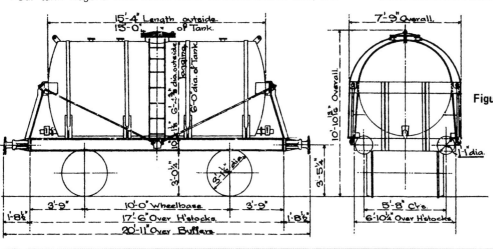

D2037
Tare: 11 tons 2 cwt 1 qr
Carrying capacity: 10 tons
A∀ and hand brakes and steam pipe
Lot 1241

Figure 163

Scale: [scale bar] feet

Plate 335 This illustrates No. 707107 with a '14.8.44' paint date on the solebar.
Photograph British Rail

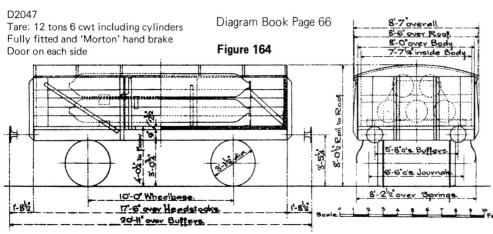

D2047
Tare: 12 tons 6 cwt including cylinders
Fully fitted and 'Morton' hand brake
Door on each side

Diagram Book Page 66

Figure 164

D2047 OXYGEN CYLINDER WAGON

Drawing number not known **Figure 164**

A number of fully fitted open wagons from D1892 were converted in 1940 and while the diagram records 8 conversions, another source records the following vehicles:-
406267/77/384/517/650/401134/264/ 308/364/564/576/401917/993.

No pictures are known to exist and it is not possible to give any further details.

SCALE |0 1 2 3 4 5 6 7 8 9 10| FEET

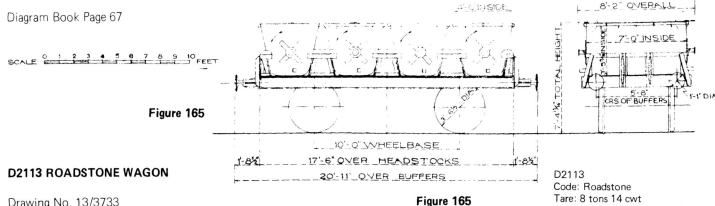

Figure 165

D2113 ROADSTONE WAGON

Drawing No. 13/3733

Built to lot 1435

A prototype vehicle No. 688000 was built in 1946 using a secondhand underframe from fish van No. 39373 which had 3'6½'' diameter wheels and Morton-type brakes with two shoes to each wheel. This vehicle is depicted in **Plate 336**.

Figure 165

D2113
Code: Roadstone
Tare: 8 tons 14 cwt
Carrying capacity per skip: 3 tons
Cubic capacity per skip: 77 cu. ft.
Weight of skip: 9 cwt 3 qrs 7 lb
'Morton' brake, AVB pipe only

Plate 336

D2131 ROADSTONE WAGON

Diagram Book Page 67A

Drawing No. 13/3799

Figure 166

Built to lot numbers 1489

Following the construction of one prototype in 1946, a further 100 vehicles were built in 1947 and 1948 carrying running numbers 688001–688100. They differed from the original

vehicle by being equipped with Morton brakes working on two wheels only and were provided with 3' 3½'' disc wheels. Comparison of **Plates 336** and **337** will show livery variations in relation to the layout along the solebar and the end construction was also different. Under British Railways ownership, they appear to have been equipped with vacuum brakes and tie rods between the 'W' irons.

SCALE |0 1 2 3 4 5 6 7 8 9 10| FEET

D2131
Code: Roadstone
Tare: 7 tons 9 cwt
Carrying capacity per skip: 3 tons
Cubic capacity per skip: 77 cu. ft.
Weight of skip: 9 cwt 3 qrs 7 lb
'Morton' brake

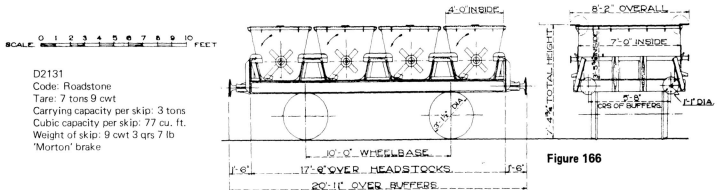

Figure 166

Plate 337 This illustrates No. 688008 in bauxite livery with a June 1947 paint date visible on the solebar.

Photograph British Rail

Plate 338 When photographed in 1964 No. 688089 had by now one pair of disc and one pair of solid spoke wheels, vacuum brakes, tie rods, different axleboxes, and is branded 'Empty to Mansfield Town'.

Photograph Author's Collection

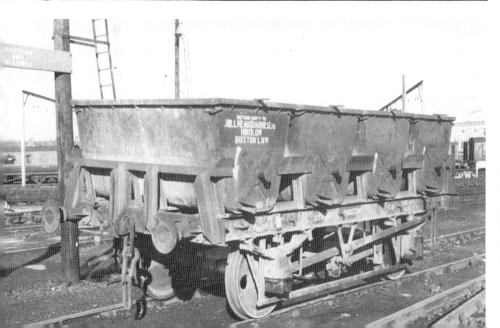

Plate 339 No. M688072 was photographed in 1964 and was also fitted with automatic vacuum brakes and tie rods, but this wagon's branding reads 'Return Empty to Hillhead Quarries Ltd Hindlow Buxton LNW'. Note the end of the pipe where the vacuum hose is normally fitted.

Photograph Author's Collection

D2114 BOCAR

Drawing No. 15/4492

Figure 167

Built to lot numbers 1487/1496

One prototype was produced in 1946 numbered 700900 and then in 1947/8 a further 35 vehicles were built numbered 700901—35. They were built upon secondhand underframes and, as will be noted on the diagram, No. 700931 was shorter in length and naturally weighed less. The author recalls block trains made up of these vehicles being worked from Birmingham Washwood Heath to Oxford via Bordesley Junction over the GWR but it cannot be stated for certain if this was their only working or if they worked elsewhere.

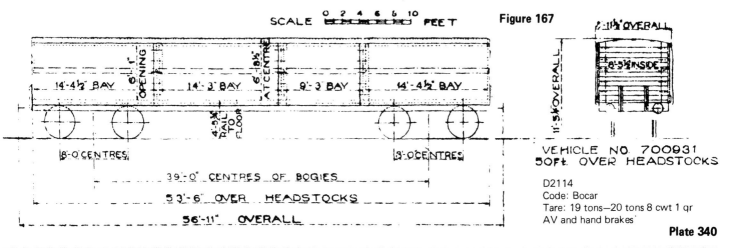

SCALE 0 2 4 6 10 FEET **Figure 167**

14'-4½' BAY — 6'-1" OPENING — 14'-3' BAY — 6'-8½' AT CENTRE — 9'-3' BAY — 14'-4½' BAY

4'-9¾' RAIL TO FLOOR

8'-0 CENTRES — 8'-0 CENTRES

39'-0" CENTRES OF BOGIES

53'-6" OVER HEADSTOCKS

56'-11" OVERALL

7'-11½' OVERALL

8'-5½' INSIDE

11'-5½' OVERALL

VEHICLE NO. 700931
50Ft. OVER HEADSTOCKS

D2114
Code: Bocar
Tare: 19 tons—20 tons 8 cwt 1 qr
AV and hand brakes

Plate 340

Plates **340** and **341** illustrate the prototype No. 700900 in both covered and uncovered condition. No doubt the ends were painted bauxite and the solebars and below black.

Photographs British Rail

Plate 341

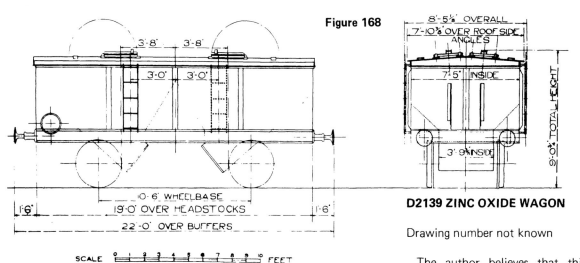

Figure 168

D2139
Tare: 10 tons
Carrying capacity: 20 tons
Cubic capacity: 524 cu. ft.
Screw hand brake
2 top door

D2139 ZINC OXIDE WAGON

Drawing number not known   **Figure 168**

The author believes that this diagram refers to the conversion in 1948 of 12 ex-GSWR hopper wagons but, unfortunately, no further information is available.

D2153   27   TON   MINERAL WAGON

Drawing No. 13/3961   **Figure 169**

A total of 400 wagons was built at Derby in 1949 and these were numbered 622100—622499 but, surprisingly, none appear to have been photographed. They would have entered traffic in grey and followed the livery style of the 16T steel mineral wagons.

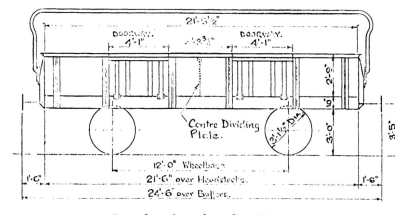

D2154
Tare: 9 tons 8 cwt
Carrying capacity: 20 tons
20 ton GWR brake

Figure 169

D2154 20 TON WAGON

Drawing number not recorded   **Figure 170**

The lot book records a total of 10 vehicles to lot 1610, comprising 20 ton wagons ex-Western Trinidad Lake Asphalt Co., dating from 1949. The author has never seen a picture of one of these wagons and is therefore unable to give any further information regarding their origin or fate in BR service.

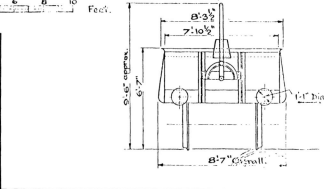

Figure 170

D2153
Code: MIN XX
Tare: 8 tons 5 cwt
Cubic capacity: 648 cu. ft.
Double brake
2 side doors, 2 flap doors, 2 bottom doors, 1 end door

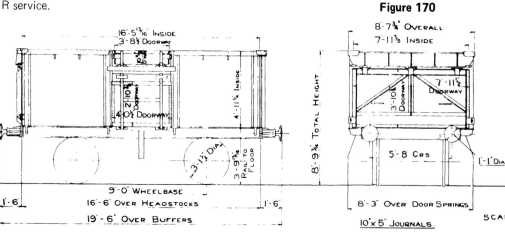

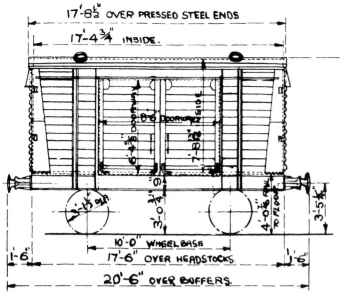

17'-8½" OVER PRESSED STEEL ENDS

17'-4¾" INSIDE.

Figure 171

10'-0" WHEELBASE
17'-6" OVER HEADSTOCKS
20'-6" OVER BUFFERS.

D2177
Tare: 7 tons 6 cwt
Double sliding doors on each side
Vehicle Nos. 508566, 508978, 508473,
altered from lot 927

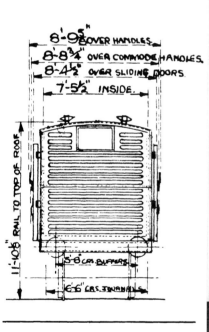

8'-9⅝" OVER HANDLES
8'-8¾" OVER COMMODE HANDLES
8'-4½" OVER SLIDING DOORS
7'-5½" INSIDE.

Figure 172

D2156
Tare: 6 tons 3 cwt
Carrying capacity: 12 tons
Double brake
2 side doors, 1 end door

16'-0" Outside
15'-6" Inside

4'-1" Doorway

9'-0" Wheelbase
16'-0" over Headstocks
19'-0" over Buffers.

D2177 GOODS VENTILATED PALLET VANS
Diagram Book Page 72

Drawing number not known   **Figure 171**

The diagram gives the details of three vans altered to provide experimental pallet vans and the solebar paint date of '22.9.50' suggests when this conversion was made.

Plate 342 No. M508978 is seen here after conversion and clearly shows the grey body livery used by BR at this time. No doubt the panels upon which the lettering was placed was black.

Photograph British Rail

Plate 342

EXPERIMENTAL   PALLET VAN

12T

M 508978

Diagram Book Page 72

D2156 12 TON HIGH GOODS WAGON

Drawing No. not known   **Figure 172**

It is interesting to note that this diagram was also given as page 72 in the diagram book (see D2177, page 72) and no explanation can be given as to why two different vehicles were given the same page number. The diagram contains all the information known about these wagons, which is rather sparse.

7'-6" Outside
7'-0" Inside

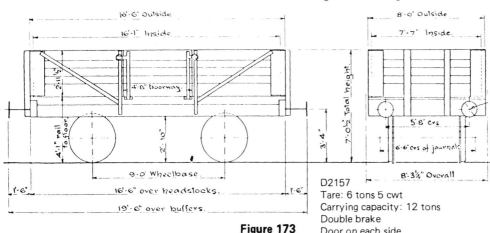

Figure 173

Scale. 0 1 2 3 4 5 6 7 8 9 10 feet.

D2157
Tare: 6 tons 5 cwt
Carrying capacity: 12 tons
Double brake
Door on each side
Part lot 1623

D2157 12 TON HIGH GOODS WAGON

Drawing number not known **Figure 173**

The lot book contains a brief entry under lot 1623, it merely states that these were 12 ton wagons from Wirksworth Quarries Ltd and does not even state how many. As with D2156 the diagram contains all the information known to the author regarding these vehicles.

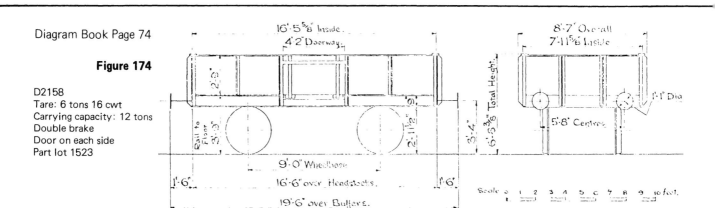

Diagram Book Page 74

Figure 174

D2158
Tare: 6 tons 16 cwt
Carrying capacity: 12 tons
Double brake
Door on each side
Part lot 1523

D2158 12 TON GOODS WAGON

Drawing number not known **Figure 174**

The remarks on page 73 D2157 wagon apply equally to D2158. Regrettably, no further information is available.

Plate 343 This picture of No. 480652 which carries a '28.12.48' paint date is the only picture known to the author.

Photograph British Rail

~ and so on to Volume 2

Specially constructed vehicles
Containers and traffic
Livery
Drawings and construction details